The Internationalization of SMEs

This volume is a product of the Interstratos project which brought together research teams across Europe to study the strategic behaviour of small and medium-sized industrial firms, with particular emphasis on their international activities.

The study took place over a period of dramatic change, including the formation of the Single European Market. It encompassed such issues as the effects of the Single Market on both those within it and outside, the influences on level of export activity, success factors, entrepreneurial types, stages in internationalization, and the effects of family ownership.

The book also contains detailed case studies of individual countries including The Netherlands, Finland, Switzerland and the UK. The combination of original research and wide ranging, original analysis should make *The Internationalization of SMEs* an invaluable text for anyone interested in the international activities of SMEs.

Editors: **Antti Haahti**, *University of Tampere*, **Graham Hall**, *Manchester Business School*, and **Rik Donckels**, *Catholic University Brussels*.

Routledge Advances in Management and Business Studies

The Internationalization of SMEs

The Interstratos project

Edited by Antti Haahti, Graham Hall and Rik Donckels

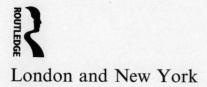

London and New York

First published 1998 by Routledge
11 New Fetter Lane, London EC4P 4EE

Simultaneously published in the USA and Canada
by Routledge
29 West 35th Street, New York, NY 10001

Typeset in Times by Puretech, India
Printed and bound in Great Britain by
TJ International, Padstow, Cornwall

British Library Cataloguing in Publication Data
A catalogue record for this book is available from
the British Library

Library of Congress Cataloguing in Publication Data
[edited by] Antti Haahti, Graham Hall and Rik Donckels
The internationalization of SMEs: the Interstratos project / p. com.
Includes bibliographical references and index.
1. International business enterprises – Europe – Case studies –
Congresses. 2. Small business – Europe – Case studies – Congresses.
3. Export marketing – Europe – Case studies – Congresses.
I. Haahti, Antti Juhani. II. Hall, Graham. III Donckels, Rik.
HD 2844.1578 1998 97–23331
338.8'884 – dc21 CIP

ISBN 0–415–13333–5

Contents

Figures

Tables

Contributors

AUSTRIA

J. Hanns Pichler
Wirtschaftsuniversität Wien

Erwin Fröhlich
Institut für Gewerbe- und Hand
werksforschung

BELGIUM

Rik Donckels
Katholieke Universiteit Brussel
Small Business Research
Institute

Ria Aerts
Katholieke Universiteit Brussel
Small Business Research Institute

FINLAND

Antti J. Haahti
School of Business Administration
University of Tampere

Petri Ahokangas
University of Oulu
Industrial Engineering and
Management

THE NETHERLANDS

Koos van Dijken
Manufacturing Industry
Department
Economisch Instituut voor het
Midden-en Kleinbedrijf
Zoetermeer

Han Gankema
Vakgroep BE
University of Groningen

Yvonne Prince
Manufacturing Industry
Department
Econimisch Instituut voor het
Midden-en Kleinbedrijf
Zoetermeer

Peter Zwart
Small Business Management
University of Groningen

NORWAY

Per-Andres Havnes,
Arild Saether
Agder College
Kristiansand

Johanne Sletten
Adger Research Foundation
Kristiansand

SWEDEN

Carin Holmquist
Department of Business
Administration
University of Umeå

Håkan Boter
Department of Business
Administration
University of Umeå

SWITZERLAND

Hans Jobst Pleitner
Schweizerisches Institut für gew.
Wirtschaft
St. Gallen

Margrit Habersaat, Jürgen
Brunner
Schweizerisches Institut für gew.
Wirtschaft
St. Gallen

UK

Graham Hall
Manchester Business School

Pete Naude
Manchester Business School

Preface

This is the first collection of papers from the Interstratos project which has been studying a wide range of aspects of small and medium-sized enterprises operating in five sectors in nine countries, though with particular attention to their international activities. There was a common core of questions but others were country specific. Most notably the British, with their usual flair for being out of step with the rest of Europe, deleted questions on values but included in their questionnaire a section on reasons for particular levels of international activity.

Authors were responsible for the contents of their papers and their views were not necessarily shared by their colleagues. Rik Donckels led the team and is now a grand master in the art of cat herding. Antti Haahti has had the onerous responsibility of producing a yearly working paper containing pooled results, together with all the other tasks no one else was willing to undertake. I was left with the easy job of smoothing the English.

Graham Hall

1 Introduction

Interstratos – a pioneering project on internationalization of SMEs in Europe

Antti Haahti

PURPOSE AND SCOPE

Interstratos (Internationalization of strategic orientations of small and medium European enterprises) is a joint research project[1] in which researchers from eight European countries cooperate in studying the international behaviour of small and medium firms. On the initiative of Rik Donckels, Erwin Fröhlich, Antti Haahti and J. Hanns Pichler our aim in the research programme is to explore international operations in manufacturing industry. So far we have amassed an extraordinary amount of data (over 5,000 observations per annum over five years) with the possibility of gaining extensive comparative insight into more than 4,000 European firms and a panel of about 800 firms.

The purpose of the longitudinal research programme is to explore patterns of internationalization and describe strategies of adjustment to changes in their task environments by small and medium manufacturing firms in Europe during the years 1991–1995. The frame of reference model is based on a broad research question: How are changes in market circumstances and task environments reflected in the changing strategic and/or situational adaptive behaviours of SMEs?

The specific research objectives are to explore and describe the following questions:

- How do changes in competitive conditions, changes in market factors and constraints and inducements to undertaking international operations influence changes in product/market strategies and especially export orientation and the degree of cooperation of small and medium manufacturing firms?
- What patterns of behaviour relevant to the modes and methods of internationalization can be observed and how do adaptive changes in this behaviour affect changes in the export success of firms?

- What kinds of resource formation in terms of learning capability can be observed in the SMEs in their growth vector from local to overseas markets and how do these learning capabilities influence their choices and mode of operations in the local market and in their international operations?
- Are changes in managers' values and attitudes related to changes in their adjustment to the demands of their task environment, and what types of learning behaviour can we observe?

To be able to observe such phenomena, five industries in different phases of evolution – growth, expansion, stability, stagnation and contraction – have been chosen and we have focussed on the patterns of adjustment of SMEs operating in food, furniture, electronics, mechanical engineering and clothing and textiles. Data from Austria, Belgium, Finland, UK, the Netherlands, Norway, Sweden and Switzerland are being collected annually over a five-year period to serve as a source of information. The objective of this book, which is meant for academic, consulting and managerial audiences, is to highlight some of the changes European SMEs have to deal with.

RESEARCH MODEL AND METHODOLOGY

Research model

Internationalization refers to the process of increasing involvement in international operations (Welch and Luostarinen 1988). Export related theories of internationalization have put forward two types of competing descriptive theories of export behaviour. The first theory concerns the stage-of-development models that are descriptions of causal patterns of development and growth. The process is viewed either as a unilinear evolutionary process with incremental steps, and characterized by sequential stages (Johanson and Wiedersheim-Paul 1975; Bilkey and Tesar 1977; Luostarinen 1979; Cavusgil *et al.* 1979; Czinkota 1983; Welch and Luostarinen 1988), or as a cyclical evolution pattern with a more differentiated character. Growth through strategic decisions is the second theory (Reid 1982, 1984; Aharoni 1966). The design of our approach allows us to test any of the competing models. We tend to lean on the strategic choice behaviour viewpoint in our research programme, but are also interested in the alternative evolutionary models.

From the outset we accept that the performance of SMEs is to a large extent dependent on external conditions, e.g. resource availability, but we also accept the view that through a planned, rational process of strategy formation a firm will increase the odds in its favour. Given less than perfect competitive conditions, it is the entrepreneur's ability to take advantage of market imperfections that determines the firm's competitive advantage. Awareness of market imperfections requires knowledge about market factors, information about market opportunities, insights into customer needs, production and products to satisfy those needs and understanding of the key success factors in the industry needed to create a sustainable position.

The basic line of thinking follows the external control theory and, therefore, we are mainly interested in the following types of relation: environment/strategic behaviour; performance/strategic behaviour. For a survey of the variables describing these relations, we refer to Table 1.1. In the next section a more detailed presentation of the variables is to be found.

Exogenous variables: the context of operations

There are quite a lot of variables that we have put forward to study. Why so many, and what is the justification for this?

The reason for such a set of variables is two-fold. First, we wish to have an opportunity to study bivariate relationships in the contingency theory fashion, and to relate, where possible, to some of these results within the contingency theory of organization literature. Second, given the limitations of bivariate contingency studies a configuration point of view will offer a more integrative approach to the study of patterns of behaviour. To succeed in such holistic studies a broad set of theoretical variables and their empirical indicators is needed.

Let us start with variables that are given to the manager such as nationality. Nationality of the responding manager is not only an indicator of domicile, but also a crude indicator of culture. If additional insights are wanted they may be gained by grouping respondents by nationality into groups such as those proposed by, for example, Hofstede (1980): (1) Germanic culture area – Austria, Switzerland and the Netherlands; (2) Scandinavian culture area – Finland, Norway and Sweden; (3) Advanced Latin culture area represented by France (France was included only once) and by Belgium (in part); and (4) Anglo cultures represented by British respondents.

Managerial characteristics that describe relevant aspects of their background such as sex, age, education, training and professional experience are listed first. The Stratos research results also suggest

Table 1.1 The variables in the model

The exogenous variables	The endogenous independent variables	The endogenous dependent variables
Manager characteristics	Corporate strategy	Business performance
Nationality	Product scope	Total sales
Age, Sex, Education	Number of product groups	Domestic sales
Work experience	Market scope	Export sales
Use of information sources	Number of customer groups	Number of employees
Manager values & attitudes	Geographic scope	
Firm and structure	Geographic location of markets	
Industry	Key success factors	
Region	Business strategy	
Size: number of employees	Export orientation	
Ownership	Import strategy	
Legal status	Form of export operations	
Degree of independence	Degree of cooperation	
Type of production		
Form of order servicing		
Contextual constraints:		
Task Environment		
Changes in competitive conditions		
Changes in market factors		
Changes in constraints & inducements		
for international operations		

that a manager's values have an important influence on all aspects of strategic behaviour and performance (Stratos 1990; Fröhlich and Pichler 1988; Haahti and Bagozzi 1994). To account, at least partially, for managers' values and attitudes a set of selected value items were included in the research design.

Knowledge about sources of knowledge may make the difference between successful and less successful performance. In the literature it is clear that there is a positive relationship between the extent of the use of information sources and successful export operations. The utilization of available information sources is assumed to favour export decisions. Ownership and related indicators will serve to differentiate between family firms and firms managed by hired managers. Recent contributions within the literature on family firms (Donckels and Fröhlich 1991) put forward the need for such a differentiation. Additionally, it is of importance to have some measure to differentiate firms managed by entrepreneurs from firms managed by hired professionals. This is of interest in attempting to specify, for example, thresholds of growth and related changes in export orientation.

The choice of industries selected for sampling was based mainly on pragmatic considerations. Most members of our team had experience of three industries (Stratos 1990), namely electronics, food, and clothing and textiles. To ascertain differences in industry growth trends, strategic behaviour and forms of international operations, mechanical engineering and furniture making were included. All these industries are sufficiently well represented in the respective countries to form a basis for international comparisons.

Size of firm is a much discussed contextual variable and indicator of structure discussed in all the relevant literature on exporting, strategic management, organizational behaviour and industrial economics. In line with the 'increase in size is related to increased specialization' hypothesis (e.g. Child 1972a) we are interested in relationships between size of firm and increasing variety in strategic behaviours. Specifically the change in size in relation to changes in export orientation is of interest (e.g. Cavusgil 1982, 1984; Reid 1984; Miesenböck 1988).

Recent advances in logistics-related information technology have caused production to become one of the determining success factors. Type of production and form of order servicing are relevant structural variables related to strategic behaviour and performance, and already pinpointed as such in the 1960s (Woodward 1965). Fast advancement and radical changes in the real time technologies of production and forms of order servicing have increased the importance of these factors as determinants of success specifically for those firms that are subcontractors, suppliers or dependent on their output quality in the market (e.g. Buffa and Sarin 1987).

Changes in conditions within market are determinants of relations between the environment, strategy and firm performance. This external control theory viewpoint is reflected in our design and we are interested in how changes in the labour, raw material and capital markets affect small business operations and export orientation.

Research into inducements and constraints on international operations is a literature of its own as it has instant practical value for training and consulting purposes. By now there is convergence in results concerning these variables within the export literature (e.g. Dichtl *et al.* 1984; Miesenböck 1988). There seem to be patterns of personal characteristics that influence changes in export orientation positively, e.g. working knowledge of foreign languages, managerial experience, level of education, sensitivity to strategic information and firm and market related factors such as size, industry, market demand, etc. Inducements and constraints are the two areas where it is felt that training and consulting services should influence export decisions favourably.

Endogenous variables: the content of operations

Next we will discuss those variables that managers can influence with their own choices and decisions.The independent endogenous variables are the following: (changes in ...) success factors, product/market strategy and international operations (we use export orientations as a synonym), and cooperation. The main dependent endogenous variables are (changes in ...) total sales, domestic sales, export sales, and number of employees.

The basic question of strategy is concerned with the question of what is produced and for whom (Ansoff 1965). The product/market choices rest on the perception of unsatisfied market needs that create profitable marketing opportunities. The purpose of the firm is to satisfy those needs and to receive an economic rent for its competitive ability at a level that covers the opportunity cost of the entrepreneur's own labour and capital input, and the opportunity cost of capital. As all firms have some combination of products and markets whereby the scope of their operations is defined, identification of that combination reveals their basic strategic choices. Numbers of product and market groups reflect the degree of specialization or diversity of the small firm. The basic alternatives are then product (line) or customer (group) specialism, or concentric or horizontal diversification.

In our study we focus on the product/market scope and key success factors variables. Export orientation and forms of cooperation are the main business strategy variables that interest us. The two latter variables might be the strategic choices of the highest order in firms with international operations and alliances as the main avenues of strategic thrust. But since they are part of the growth vector component of strategy, we will regard them as business strategies.

Product/market choices and success factors are intimately intertwined. Identifying and weighing the importance of key success factors relative to competitors is at the core of corporate strategy analysis. Key success factors are those variables that managers can influence to gain an advantageous competitive position in their industry, and these variables are derived from the interaction of the economic and technological characteristics of the industry and the competitive weaponry used in that industry.

In the Interstratos study we are interested in the key success factors as a basis for export strategy. Managers of SMEs are not omnipotent. There is often a scarcity of management capability, information management capacity, knowledge of markets, logistics, distribution, etc., that requires some form of cooperation with other firms to combine forces. This building of strategic mosaics becomes more important in order to respond to the opportunities now opening with the growth of the European home market.

In our study of how entrepreneurs' decisions determine patterns of trade (Thomas and Araujo 1986) we focus on changes in forms of international operations. The alternative forms of operation have often been studied in connection with the phases of international operations, which generally distinguish at least four stages of involvement: no regular export activities; export via agents; overseas sales subsidiary; and foreign production and manufacturing (see for example Johanson and Wiedersheim-Paul 1975; Luostarinen 1979). Recording the alternative forms of operationalization enables the degree of international involvement to be identified.

Since it is assumed that businessmen are not always aware of international opportunities, it is of interest to investigate what sources of information patterns are associated with export orientation. Small size may represent a possible disadvantage and a major obstacle in pursuing foreign opportunities (e.g. Reid 1982). As the results are mixed and often contradictory due to problems in defining size and measuring the effects, this question remains unresolved. Likewise the interesting question about size and whether there are thresholds in the growth of a firm after which the likelihood of exporting increases significantly remains unanswered.

Methodology

In the following sections the underlying sample design, procedures for data collection as well as processing, and approaches toward data analysis are discussed.

Sample design

The population for this study includes small and medium-sized manufacturing firms in Europe, in size classes 1–9, 10–19, 20–49, 50–99, and 100–499 employees, in the food, textiles and clothing, electrical engineering and electronics, furniture making and mechanical engineering industries. The population universe was accessed through countrywise sampling frames consisting of individual firms (varying between 1–500 employees) as sampling units, and listed in national statistical bureaus or other similar sources where available. The sampling procedure was random sampling stratified by industry and size class with a minimum quota for each cell. The quotas for each cell are of 20 observations every year that are to be followed through for five years. To achieve this, large enough original samples have to be drawn to account for the probable loss or termination of panel members.

A longitudinal panel study[2] is differentiated here from repeated cross-section data in that the focus of the panel study is on the changes in the variables of interest observed in the same, identified firms over a predetermined time. Thus, we wish to observe and describe changes in specific variables in identified firms over a few years.

A master questionnaire was developed through a detailed outline of variables listed in English followed by a German questionnaire tested in the Austrian pilot study (1990). This was then translated into all participating languages, i.e. Dutch, Finnish, French, Norwegian, and Swedish. In some questionnaires there are country-specific questions.

The main study was started by a two-wave postal survey during the first year (1991). As can be seen in Table 1.2 the total number of observations was 5,668 (1991: $N = 3,243$) firms contacted in the eight countries during the second year 1992. The total number of observations in each cell of the size classes is within the acceptable range in each industry sampled. There is a 1 to 3 ratio in sample sizes between the smallest and largest sample in size classes. Specifically, the smallest firms (0–9 employees) are over-represented as we are most interested in that part of the SME population.

Table 1.2 Interstratos sample by size, class and country (2nd survey, 1992)

	Textiles/ clothing	Electronics	Food	Industry Furniture making	Mechanical engineering	Totals
Size						
0–9 employees	438	282	326	418	450	1,914
10–19 employees	151	145	191	234	350	1,071
20–49 employees	207	180	202	246	405	1,240
50–99 employees	95	127	142	113	275	752
100–499 employees	96	118	164	71	242	691
Country						
Austria	257	84	261	323	305	1,230
Belgium	45	27	50	52	66	240
Finland	70	67	78	48	140	403
France	41	25	36	30	58	190
Netherlands	208	292	191	233	690	1,614
Norway	57	55	74	78	93	357
Sweden	154	161	161	139	226	841
Switzerland	93	81	99	114	82	469
UK	65	69	78	67	66	345
Total	990	861	1,028	1,084	1,726	5,668

Since these populations are dynamic, in some industries there is strong growth and in some others the effect of the early 1990s depression is seen in decreasing sizes of industry populations. The weighting of data is considered annually.

Analytical aspects

The choice of alternative analytical approaches is dependent upon the questions we propose to investigate. Therefore, to get meaningful insights from the data analysis is carried out on several levels, such as the industry, size of firm and the nationality of the respondent.

Since we are interested in all aspects of internationalization, a broader classification of stages of internationalization is proposed:

• domestic firm, no imports;
• domestic firm, imports;
• irregular exports;

- regular exports;
- licensing; and
- direct investment with different modes of operation.

This will retain the stages-of-development model which is a useful approach for further classification of the sample into more meaningful subsets for further analysis.

The panel study allows for both cross sectional and longitudinal variations in the analyses. Often the reliability and stability of key variables is of interest. There are several approaches to analysing panel data such as test/retest and structural equation modelling. The test/retest method is affected by several shortcomings. For example, a simple test/retest correlation is affected by random measurement errors as well as temporal instability of the variable. A distinction is not made between observation and latent variables even when one assumes that variables are measured perfectly.

A method provided to separate stability and reliability of the (latent) variables is to explicitly model the measurement errors. Structural equation models provide for such an opportunity. The main alternatives are single-indicator multiple-wave models, multiple-indicator multiple-wave models and other models offering explanations for serially correlated errors. But as this report is on the whole concerned mainly with the 1991 and 1992 results, we will not go further into this topic.

A REVIEW OF THE PAPERS IN THE BOOK

The theory of internationalization processes is examined and applied to small firms in this first collection of papers to cover the results of the Interstratos research project. The paper by Boter and Holmquist differs from all the rest in that their fundamental view – the multilevel approach – attached significant explanatory importance to such factors as integration of cultural, political, and market conditions and management as potential explanatory forces in describing the sequential process of internationalization. They prepared six case studies of companies in the Scandinavian countries of Finland, Norway, and Sweden. The companies formed two categories: conventional and innovative companies. Some of these case companies were included in the research group's longitudinal data set.

Two distinct forms of processes for internationalization were found: the innovative companies' global focus on a narrow product scope and superior technological cum managerial competence, and the conventional companies' local focus on production-oriented manufacturing culture. Contrary to the original expectation that national differences would exist, few were found. Instead a striking similarity among the companies in each category, conventional and innovative, was evident. The differences between conventional and innovative companies were evident on industry, company and individual levels. This established also a justification for the chosen analytical approach so evident in the rest of papers that heavily concentrate on rather distinct, item-level phenomena and partial descriptive and analytical models.

The decision to stay outside the European Union did have implications for the international strategies of Swiss companies. According to Pleitner, Brünner and Habersaat it is evident that Swiss SMEs have started to operate more outside Europe, in the USA and in Asia rather than within the Union. At the same time larger Swiss companies are among the biggest buyers of companies within the EU. In their paper the authors focus on the factors that have increased the probability of success of Swiss companies given new competitive disadvantage in European markets. To confront these new threats, the companies' need to reposition has increased dramatically.

In the Swiss contribution the focus is on success factors. Distinctive competencies are critical internal resources of any firm. The ability of the management is measured when distinctive competencies are matched with key success factors in the market. The match is a complex process of learning. It means awareness of both opportunities and threats in the task environment. It requires capability to match the perceived opportunities with the strengths of the firm. It requires the capability to become aware and eliminate the shortcomings in its resources.

Awareness about external changes that threaten to spoil any advantages the firm may have is required by every successful entrepreneur. One either adapts to changing circumstances, finds a niche where changes do not have any manageable influence, or attempts to alter the circumstances. The pioneers and innovators do the last, most other firms hope to be efficient allocators and successful in adapting.

This problem of strategic match, and the importance of key success factors to the future of the company was studied in their paper by Pleitner, Brünner and Habersaat in relation to stages of internationalization of Swiss SMEs. For some time, being excluded from the EU has been seen as a serious threat to Swiss market share in the European Union. Price, quality, technology, foreign competitors, cooperation and concentration is seen as intensifying the competition. The markets have to be found globally, and the study indicates that there is a marked increase in Swiss activities outside the European market. A stream of activities is directed to the Pacific Rim, and Asian markets. A combinatory approach to international modes of operations is often evident. Almost 70 per cent utilize a combination of three or more approaches to operations in international markets.

Of the key success factors that are seen as most important the following clearly stand out: the reliability of delivery; flexibility; and product quality combined with after sales services. Other key success factors of high importance are: quality of management; workers' skills; local image; and customer relations. Market share, on the contrary, is seen as of least importance, mainly due to the fact that SMEs most often are small share operators in the market. To sum up, half of the 19 success factors tested were consistently perceived as of importance, and these were: product quality; reliability of delivery; flexibility; management quality; worker' skills; customer service; local image; quality of sales staff; ability to solve technical problems; and customer relations. What comes out of the study with certainty is that SMEs are well on their way to become international operators.

In their study of types of entrepreneurs Fröhlich and Pichler created a theoretically based typology tested and characterized empirically by the value structures of European entrepreneurs from eight countries. The Stratos study, on which this was based, preceded the present Interstratos study. The typology consisted of four entrepreneurial types – pioneers, organizers, allrounders, routineers. Pioneers are the basic Schumpeterian pioneer entrepreneurs who are those who, as innovators, may fundamentally change the market supply and demand conditions. Organizers and allrounders represent the Leibnitzean view of the efficient allocater who is needed to apply the, sometimes revolutionary, innovations of the pioneers of any field. This dimensionality in behaviour – innovative pioneering internally controlled behaviour, and adaptive, externally controlled behaviour – is a fundamental continuum that also described differences in entrepreneurial behaviour very well.

Therefore, it is interesting and justifiable in Interstratos to consider the possibility of differentiating between the internationalization behaviors of these basic types of entrepreneurs/managers. Fröhlich & Pichler do not avail themselves of the total set of 84 value items that were used in the previous Stratos study, but use a scale of 12 value items that distinguished most between the two basic types – pioneers and organizers. After cluster analysis of the total annual data of Interstratos they describe the differences between the two types among a few interesting descriptive and background variables.

It is interesting to note that there are consistent differences in the means for the following values and attitude statements for country, industry and size of the firm:

- 'jobs should be clearly described and defined in detail';
- 'managers should plan rather than follow their intuition';
- 'firms should only introduce proven office procedures and production techniques';
- 'changes in business should be avoided at all costs'; and
- 'a firm should not leave the region where it is established'.

Pioneers seemed to be mostly in disagreement with these statements whereas organizers agreed or strongly agreed. In terms of a statement – 'should managers consider ethical behaviour in their decision making' most agreed.

In this context it is of importance to note that there is a minority that do not consider it necessary to consider ethical principles in daily affairs. The minority varies in terms of percentage of the total sample from 2 per cent up to 15 per cent. There are national differences here which beg for further in-depth investigations.

The aim of Interstratos is to provide opportunities for cutting-edge research into reviewing, testing and modifying theories, as these concern both stage theories and process theories of the internationalization of the firm. Several criteria have to be met in such an attempt. Before longitudinal testing there must be a thorough discussion of the relevant models and their strengths and shortcomings. The group of models that Ahokangas has focused on are the resource theories of firm. An accepted view within the field is that the extent and form of internationalization is dependent on the external conditions, i.e. the external resource availability. The availability of external resources is thus an exogenous independent variable. In the literature two forms of behaviour are often linked with external resources: the ability and capacity for cooperating within your own country to form networks or alliances for foreign operations; and the interest in and active search for external sources of information. Information search, learning and networking for competitive advantage seem to account for important external resource acquirement behaviour.

International orientation – the scope of international activities, the stage of international operations, and the complexity of international operations – is the endogenous explanatory variable in his model that explains the success in international operations measured here with the employee weighted export sales, and the percentage of exports from total sales.

The subsample consists of 328 Scandinavian firms from the 1993 crossection. A four-factor model (orientation, information use, co-operation, export strategy – accounting for 80 per cent of the variance in the subsample) was prepared in order to cluster the behaviour patterns. The resulting four exclusive types of international strategic behaviour offer a fresh insight into international patterns of the behaviour of SMEs. The clusters were starters, learning, dependent and advanced. Viewing the extent of internationalization from the resource based view assumes that internationalization should be seen as the development of a firm's resources through interaction within a network. The model is now being tested with five-year panel data that became available while this book was being written.

Havnes, Sletten and Saether were interested in the question of north–south regional differences. The differences in export activity due to regional location are investigated in the paper that links its research objective to the early study of Chenerey, Clark and Cao-Pinna that studied the regional structure of the Italian economy. This time the focus is on the differences in export activity of firms operating in the common Nordic Calott area (consisting of the three most northerly areas of Finland, Norway and Sweden) in comparison with those that operate in the southern regions of the respective countries. Regional structure is given, not studied *per se*. But it is the locational difference that is of interest.

In the Italian study the economic strength of the northern regions explained the more positive indirect effects of investment programmes meant for the advancement of the southern industrial regions. The Nordic Calott area has always been the most subsidized area in Scandinavia. But whether there is a connection between location and export orientation was the relevant question explored by the authors. The sets of variables used to describe the possible differences were: firm location; management characteristics; market contact; and distance in association with export propensity.

Clear differences in export propensity due to location were found when contrasting exporters with non-exporters. The most important intervening variable seems to be firm characteristics, i.e. firm size and industry sector. There is an increase in the probability of being an exporter given southern location. Given increase in size of firm, this difference disappears.

Fewer or no differences were found in terms of export rate. Export rate is related to the industry sectors in the countries. It is obvious that the other Scandinavian countries are the important targets for exports. The neighbourhood psychology strengthens ties for business.

Trade with neighbouring countries is more important than the size of their respective economies would indicate. Reasons that come to mind are lower transportation costs, shorter psychic distance and traditionally open Nordic markets. Neither should the effect of the structural differences between the industries of the three countries be overlooked.

Due to their geographic central location the Dutch industries have traditionally been internationalized or rather globalized in their character. Prince and van Dijken address two questions: what are the deteriminants for exporting and non-exporting; and what are the determinants for the ratio of export sales to total sales, ie. the determining factors for the extent of exporting.

Given the first question, there are in the literature several sets of determinants that explain the difference in export–non-export behaviours, such as both external and internal stimuli e.g. managements' export expectations, management commitment, differential firm advantages and managerial aspirations, characteristics of the environment, strategic variables and functional variables. Most often these studies concentrate on item level indicators as the variables analysed. The four last mentioned were used in this study of the 1991 Dutch data with 175 exporting firms and 215 non-exporting firms.

The results for the first question indicate that the three most discriminating factors between exporters and non-exporters are emphasis on competitive strategies, firm size (number of employees) and ability to use foreign languages. Non-exporters' firm size mean was about 17 employees whereas exporters had on average 77 employees. The probability of being an exporter increases with the number of languages available (active exporters communicate in three languages, on average), and with strong emphasis on competitive strategies and limited liability in business form.

The extent of export performance was the second question asked. In addition to the discriminating factors studied in the first question, several other variables hypothesized in previous studies to have influence, were tested. The extent of exports, the export quote, is influenced by management characteristics such as the number of languages spoken, number of weeks spent abroad, active search behaviour for export orders, type of production, ie. series production and/or production to stock, and by presence of subsidiaries abroad. The increase in size of the firm does not seem to influence the increase in the proportion of exports to total sales. Other factors account for that phenomenon.

The important question of the influence of chosen international strategies on performance is studied by Gankema, Zwart and van Dijken. In comparing the Dutch and Finnish international operations they looked for strategies that seemed to be successful, what strategy patterns were observed and how they related to performance, and to the country of origin of the firm. Extending the Priest model of primary strategies (e.g. Ansoff development strategies) and secondary strategies (e.g. Porter and Kotler's basic strategies that relate to task environment) to an international context, an interesting hierarchy of strategies with four levels is proposed as the structured approach to internationalization.

The four levels of the hierarchy of strategies consisted of: (1) Ansoff product/market strategies, i.e. alternative growth paths of any firm (namely, market penetration, product development, market development or diversification); (2) Porter's generic strategies (differentiation, focus, cost leadership); (3) Wind, Douglas and Perlmutter's model of strategic dispositions in market orientation, i.e. alternatives in geographic segmentation (ethnocentrism, polycentrism, regiocentrism and geocentrism which here was understood as global orientation); and (4) entry strategy (no export, indirect export, direct export, joint ventures, license, direct investment).

When clustering was conducted on each hierarchic level, distinctly different patterns between Finnish and Dutch firms were identified. The most frequent paths of firms and their differences were observed and analysed. In the Netherlands the combination of market penetration-focus-ethnocentric-no export is the most frequent strategy combination, whereas in Finland the combination international market development-focus-polycentric-direct export is the most common. The combinations were, however, not very successful.

The question of family versus non-family influences in international business is discussed in Donckels and Aerts' paper. It is factually true that a considerable portion of the SMEs that are active on the international scene are family businesses. The literature would suggest family businesses are, however, more conservative and less active in their strategic international behaviours. Accordingly, the authors found that family businesses were clearly proportionally less active on the international scene on any of the alternative types of operation observed. The family matters in running an international business.

Changes over time of various aspects of the strategic management of British SMEs are considered by Hall and Naude. Though there are some notable exceptions, the overall conclusion to be drawn from their results is that little had changed in the perceptions of owners of SMEs about the conditions facing their companies, about the factors associated with their success and about their reasons for exporting or not exporting.

NOTES

1 The international group of research known as Interstratos group consisted in 1991 of J. Hanns Pichler, Erwin Fröhlich, Inge Fröhlich and Peter Voithofer (Austria), Rik Donckels and Ria Aerts (Belgium), Graham Hall (Great Britain), Antti Haahti, Allan Lehtimäki and Petri Ahokangas (Finland), Rob van der Horst, Koos van Dijken, Ro Braaksma (The Netherlands), Per-Andres Havnes, Arlid Saether, Johanne Sletten (Norway), Håkan Boter, Carin Holmquist (Sweden), Hans Jobst Pleitner and Margrit Habersaat (Switzerland).
2 The exception being the UK study. This did not rely on panel data.

REFERENCES

Aharoni, Y. (1966) *The Foreign Investment Decision Process*, Boston, MA: Harvard University Press.
Ansoff, I. (1965) *Corporate Strategy*, New York: McGraw-Hill.
Bilkey, W.J. and Tesar, G. (1977) 'The Export Behaviour of Smaller-Sized Wisconsin Manufacturing Firms', *Journal of International Business Studies*, 8: 93–8.
Buffa, E.S. and Sarin, R.K. (1987) *Modern Production & Operations Management*, New York: Wiley.
Cavusgil, S.T. (1982) 'Some Observations on the Relevance of Critical Variables for Internationalization Stages', in M. Czinkote & G. Tesar (eds) *Export Management: An International Context*, New York: Praeger.
Cavusgil, S.T. (1984) 'Differences Among Exporting Firms Based on their Degree of Internationalization', *Journal of Business Research*, 12: 195–208.
Cavusgil, S.T., Bilkey, W.J. and Tesar, G. (1979) 'A Note on the Export Behaviour of Firms: Export Profiles', *Journal of International Business Studies*, 10(2): 91–7.
Child, J. (1972a) 'Organizational Structures, Environment and Performance: The Role of Strategic Choice', *Sociology*, 6, 1: 2–22.
Czinkota, M.R. (1983) 'The Export Development Process: A Validation Inquiry', Staff Paper No. 4. Georgetown University, quoted by J. Stranskov in P. Buckley & P. Ghauri, (eds) *The Internationalization of The Firm*, London: Academic Press.
Dichtl, E., Leibold, M., Köglmayr, H-G and Müller, S. (1984) 'The Export Decision of Small and Medium-sized Firms: A Review', *Management International Review*, 24,2: 49–59.
Donckels, R. and Fröhlich, E. (1991) 'Sind Familienbetriebe Wirklich Anders?' Internationales Gewerbearchiv, Häfte 4, St. Gallen-Berlin, pp. 219 ff.
Fröhlich, E. and Pichler, J.H. (1988) *Werte und Typen Mittelständischer Unternehmer*. Beitrage zur Ganzheitlichen Wirtschafts- und Gesellschaftslehre. Band 8, Berlin: Duncker & Humboldt.
Haahti, A. and Bagozzi, R.P. (1994) 'Die Strategische Orientierung von Klein- und Mittelunternehmen: Die Auswirkung von Manager – Werhaltungen auf Strategie und Leistungen', Internationales Gewerbearchiv: Zeitschrift für Klein- und Mittelunternehmen. 3 Heft, 42 Jahrgang.
Hofstede, G. (1980) *Culture's Consequences*, London: Sage Publications.
Johanson, J., Wiedersheim-Paul, F. (1975) 'The Internationalization of the Firm: Four Swedish cases', *Journal of Management Studies*, 12, 3: 305–22.

Luostarinen, R. (1979) *The Internationalization of The Firm*, Acta Academiae Oeconomiae Helsingiensis, A:30.

Miesenböck, K.J. (1988) 'Small Business and Exporting: A Literature Review', *International Small Business Journal*, 6,2: 42–58.

Reid, S. (1982) 'The Impact of Size on Export Behaviour in Small Firms', in M. Czinkota and G. Tesar (eds) *Export Management: An International Context*, New York: Praeger pp. 18–38.

Reid, S. (1984) 'Market Expansion and Firm Internationalization', in E. Kaynak (ed.) *International Marketing Management*, New York, pp. 197–206.

Stratos Group (1990), *Strategic Orientations of Small European Business*, Avebury, Aldershot: Gower Publishing,

Thomas, M.J. and Araujo, L. (1986) 'Export Behaviour: Directions for Future Research', in P.W. Turnbull and S.J. Paliwoda, *Research in International Marketing*, pp. 138–61.

Welch, L.S. and Luostarinen, R. (1988) 'Internationalization: Evolution of a Concept', *Journal of General Management*, 14, 2.

Woodward, J. (1965) *Industrial Organization: Theory and Practice*, London: Oxford University Press.

2 Industry characteristics and internationalization processes in small firms[1]

Håkan Boter and Carin Holmquist

SUMMARY

The purpose of this study of small firms is to compare the process of internationalization in traditional manufacturing companies with corresponding processes in companies oriented toward innovation. Case studies were conducted in six small Nordic companies: three conventional and three innovative. The underlying concept of the conventional companies is strictly production oriented. Investment in engineering workshops and an effective organization for production constitute their most important strategy. In the innovative companies the production equipment is relatively easy to move, and over the years these companies have changed the location of their production plants a number of times. The basic meaning of technology also differs in the two categories of industry. The conventional companies are based on an established technology that can be purchased through well-known market channels. In the innovative companies the process of developing new products or serving as an intermediary between research organizations and end users demands close contact with people and organizations close to the technological core of the industry.

The conventional companies are incorporated as a multidimensional industrial system of suppliers, competitors, and other companies, and the individual companies within these industries are constrained by the rules dictated by these networks. The innovative companies all have a concentrated product scope, which implies that it is relatively easy to achieve efficiency in various functions such as R&D, production, and marketing activities. This clear distinction between functions has been advantageous to the process of internationalization.

The conventional companies have characteristics typical of family-controlled companies, i.e. the management team consists of a handful of people often closely associated with the owner family. The observation on the industry level that the game is governed by some very rigid rules is also evident on the management level, where the significant people are always kept within narrow limits. The individuals in the innovative companies have a very high level of education; they work in teams together with partners from other companies and/or organizations and they adhere to high professional standards.

The results from these six case studies indicate that the internationalization process must be understood in the context of the industry, company, and people involved. International trade and cooperation will most certainly increase. Therefore it is important to observe that the conditions for industries and single companies are different. Conventional companies have a natural local concentration that ultimately implies different strategies from the innovative companies that have a global focus.

INTRODUCTION

Business is becoming increasingly international. This is true for large as well as for small companies, even if the former often have longer experience. This paper analyses differences in the internationalization process of a sample of small companies. The aim of the analysis is to find out whether the process follows a sequential pattern, as is argued in some studies (Aharoni 1966; Johanson and Wiedersheim-Paul 1975) or whether it has developed rapidly and in giant leaps, as others argue (Hedlund and Kverneland 1984; Lindqvist 1991). A further aim is to discover whether the differences between nations, with regard to management styles, as indicated by studies of large firms (Bartlett and Ghoshal 1989; Calori and de Woot 1994) also exist for smaller firms.

Six small Nordic companies form the primary empirical basis for this study. Three are established companies with a traditional manufacturing profile; three are young, very innovative and internationally active. We propose that traditional business activities (in terms of an industrial base and a mature company structure) in the case of the small firm implies a lengthy and organized process of internationalization. We also propose that a company in a sector characterized by high-technology demands (with first-generation products and with a pronounced internal start-up climate) will experience a more rapid process of internationalization wherein the development of various functions does not follow a predictable order. The main results of the study support these proposals. Our conclusion is that research into internationalization in small firms must study the environment in which the companies are operating. A further conclusion is that the history and the internal situation of the company strongly influence the internationalization process in a small firm. The fact that small firms are heavily dependent on factors in the environment and have a limited internal resource capacity means that the units of analysis must be based on a comprehensive view that includes the industry, the company, and the individuals.

Theoretical work on the internationalization process in companies is extensive, but it is difficult to find any characteristic common to all the approaches. Instead, the field can be described as being rather fuzzy (Bartlett and Ghoshal 1991; Melin 1992). Numerous studies have analyzed the internationalization process in terms of company strategy, company structures and links to environmental conditions. Aharoni (1966) studied the decision process in companies involved in international investments and has found that coincidences and opportunities were often the most important factors in the process of internationalization. Studies of export behaviour have found that international activities within a company start with irregular foreign sales. As the involvement in foreign activities increases, sales units will be established abroad; the final step will be a production unit in another country (Johanson and Vahlne 1977; Johanson and Wiedesheim-Paul 1975). Other similar approaches analyse internationalization as a rational process successively tying management and other resources within the company to international operations. Cavusgil (1980) for example defined five stages in the process to which critical activities linked, activities that the company must cope with in order to be able to develop the process of internationalization.

The stage theory of internationalization has been widely used in empirical research, and many studies have confirmed the validity of the findings. The situation in many small firms substantiates the finding that the process of internationalization is very lengthy and incremental. Small firms usually sell the major part of their production on the domestic market (Boter and Holmquist 1994), and their limited resource base implies that export activities must be planned far ahead, often in cooperation with service organizations and other companies (Andersson and Lundin 1992).

However, some critics think that a successive development process is most valid in the initial phase and that small as well as giant leaps in the chain of development are more frequent (Hedlund and Kverneland 1984). Others say simply that the model must be replaced by one based on specific knowledge about the company and business environment to gain better understanding and explanation of the internationalization behaviour of the individual companies (Nordström 1991). In a study of small companies (Gandemo and Andersson 1993) the results gave no indication that the decision to invest in a foreign country is a step in a process where such investment is preceded by an established export to that country. Bilkey and Tesar (1977) showed that export by small firms does not necessarily mean that the effort is concentrated on one or a few markets or countries, which would be in line with the stage theory of internationalization. Instead small firms can choose to penetrate a number of markets selected rather randomly. Nevertheless, the stage approach can be a useful platform when studying internationalization in small firms that belong to conventional manufacturing industries. The limited resource base in this type of small company implies that the process of being involved in foreign activities, in terms of export, cooperation with other companies, R&D investments, etc., must be gradual and executed in incremental steps over a long period of time.

At the same time, studies have shown that knowledge-intensive or high tech small firms behave very differently and that the process of internationalization can be instant and less organized (Lindqvist 1991).

Since internationalization processes involve many different levels, inside and outside the company, it is essential to understand the dynamics between these levels. This is especially true for small companies where the role of the individual, often an entrepreneur, is vital for the process of internationalization. Before presenting and analysing six case studies, we will therefore discuss in more detail internationalization as a multilevel process, where strategic management must include individual, company, industry and national aspects.

A MULTILEVEL APPROACH

Coordination of strategic business functions in different cultural settings is a prerequisite for survival in international business. However, only a few studies have aimed to integrate management and the cultural dimension (Lyles 1990). Some theories emphasize how important it is for the company to consider political aspects, cultural factors within a country and market conditions. Although studies have also been made of the linkages between the strategic image of the company and the corporate culture, only in exceptional cases has there been any theoretical integration of these two areas (Prahalad and Doz 1987; Whitley 1992).

The field of culture in theoretical work is treated in a very heterogeneous manner. Aspects of company culture, cultures of regions, culture of industries, etc., are mixed with dimensions of national culture and used in an endeavour to understand company behaviour better. Inasmuch as the social, economic, and political environments of countries define the fundamental conditions for international business activities, we consider such dimensions of the national culture to be the metaframework. Within this national culture framework, the importance of values and norms within industries and companies must be observed in combination with the role of individuals. Below we discuss central cultural aspects of nation, industry, company, and individual in the context of international business.

There is a wide variety of research focusing on national culture (Tayed 1988). One of the most frequently cited in this field is Hofstede (1980), who studied a large multinational company and presented a model for operationalizing central aspects of national culture. Hofstede found that countries differed in work-related issues in the fields of power distance, degree of collectivism, degree of uncertainty avoidance and masculinity/femininity. The Aston group (Hickson and MacMillan 1981) has a long tradition of analysing a large number of external and internal factors with the aim of providing indications about organizational archetypes.

Important variables according to these findings are the characteristics of the national culture. Adler (1986) also studies national differences and attributes them to some basic notions, for instance how time is viewed.

The term industry is frequently used to classify individual companies on the basis of a set of common characteristics mainly related to types of product, production technology or market attributes. These industries are often analysed on a high level of aggregation, such as the competitive advantage of nations, including industrial strategies for the business sector (Sölvell *et al.* 1991). The approach underlines the importance of linking the analysis of the company and the specific sector to which it belongs (Child 1988; Turner 1971), and many studies certify that today most industrial sectors are exposed to international competition (Porter 1986, 1990). A concentration on business sectors is also found in studies that focus on R&D activities and the use of high tech applications. A company of this kind may have an intensive international network to enable it to exchange technological information in a fast-moving sector of the economy. Many of these high tech companies are small (Klofsten 1992). Finally we have the so-called network theories that focus on industrial systems and the structure and operations within such systems. Small firms are frequently involved in industrial systems with actors from a number of industries or as only one participant in a cooperative network of small firms (Johanson and Mattson 1988; Sharma 1991; Nilsson and Nilsson 1992). The corporate culture on the company level has long been in focus. The spirit and image of the company is stressed, and various cultural styles of business, leadership and organization are discussed (Deal and Kennedy 1982). In management theory organizational culture has become one of the more prominent structural variables to be matched with the appropriate strategy. The corporate culture can also be linked with the value system of an organization. The norms and values of individuals, together with the values of the significant actors, form the dominant concept of values within the organization. These values will change continuously; sometimes a company has a multicultural concept, i.e. different sets of values and ideas exist side by side (Stymne 1970; Ansoff 1979; Frost *et al.* 1985). In the small firm the organization is thinner both vertically and horizontally. One person, the owner-manager, together with a small leadership team, will often have a strong influence over the activities. This narrow resource base will not only limit the production technology but also the organization of marketing, sales and R&D.

In small firms there is a variety of reasons for paying extra attention to the role of the individuals. The small organization is often dominated by a few people, and the educational level, work experience, etc. of this group can provide substantial explanation for the actions of the company (Kornadt *et al.* 1980; Jahoda 1992). The professional culture in many small, knowledge-intensive companies is characterized by the strong professional identity of the participant individuals.

In summary, the national culture represents the specific setting of language, values, norms, etc. in a country that is of ultimate importance for international strategic management. Within the frame of a national culture, every company is in turn involved in a cultural context typical of the specific industry. Furthermore, every organization has a company culture and on the individual level certain people, some with culturally different traits, are significant actors in the activities of the company. This line of reasoning implies that cultural aspects are important for the internationalization process, and that these aspects are seen on many levels. Because we are interested in comparing companies in three countries and companies in different types of business (conventional and innovative) we need to study internationalization processes on all the levels mentioned above: nation; industry; company; and individual. We argue, consequently, that a multilevel approach to studying the process of internationalization in small firms is preferable.

THE PROCESS OF INTERNATIONALIZATION: SIX CASE STUDIES

Using an explorative approach we have carried out case studies of six small companies in three Nordic countries. Our aim was to analyse management styles found in different countries, and to this end the six companies selected are evenly spread over Norway, Sweden and Finland. Because earlier results in our studies indicated that small firms in the Nordic countries form a rather homogeneous group within the European context, we wanted to analyse further those country differences that nevertheless existed.

All six companies sell some part of their production to another country. Earlier experience from theoretical and empirical studies generated the hypothesis that the process of internationalization in small firms is relatively lengthy and follows a logical incremental process in traditional manufacturing companies but can be very rapid and disorganized in younger companies belonging to the high tech or knowledge-intensive sectors. In order to differentiate between various types of company we deliberately chose to split the studied population into two such groups. The first group comprises traditional manufacturing companies active in an old/mature (at least 15 years old) industrial sector and using an established production technology. The second group is made up of relatively newly established companies whose production is based on high technology or new technological solutions. We named these groups 'conventional' and 'innovative', respectively. One of each type was selected in Norway, Sweden and Finland. The background data for the companies are presented in Tables 2.1 and 2.2.

Table 2.1 Three case studies – conventional companies

	Norway	*Sweden*	*Finland*
Name	AS Kristiansands Skruefabrik	Polar & Sävsjö AB	OMP-Konepaja Oy
Industry	Mechanical engineering	Transport sector, caravans	Heavy metal constructions
Location	South of Norway – heavily industrial offshore district	North of Sweden – sparsely populated area	North of Finland – medium-sized town, university and forest industry
Employees	80	47	50
Exports	5%	20%	30%
Export channels	Agents and personal networks	Sales offices in the Nordic countries	Personal networks

The interviews with the managing directors of all companies were taped. Additional material collected included annual reports, project documentation and contracts. We were quite familiar with the Swedish companies from previous research projects. The interviews and in-depth questions were formulated to cover company history, current situation, internationalization process, management and cultural aspects in the business. We present first the three conventional companies, then the three innovative, in Norway, Sweden and Finland, respectively.

The family-controlled Kristiansands Skruefabrik AS, founded in 1918, manufactures mechanical products mainly as subcontractor to the offshore and shipyard industry in the southern part of Norway. Short-term orders imply frequent changes and tailor-made operations, and the 80 employees must be highly qualified in industrial metal work. Direct export is low, but via the offshore industry the indirect involvement can be very intensive for some projects. Sweden is the only foreign country where Kristiansands Skruefabrik has realized international projects in terms of exhibitions and cooperation with large companies. The cultural differences between Norway and Sweden are described as very small and easy to cope with. Differences in regional dimensions such as urban areas and rural regions seem to be more important than national characteristics. The managing director pointed out that people working in the same profession often share an effective means of communicating irrespective of national origin.

Polar & Sävsjö AB, was founded in 1988 after a merger between two independent companies producing caravans. Polar started thirty years ago in a sparsely populated area in northern Sweden and became one of the most important players on the national market. Sävsjö also started in the 1960s as a company importing English caravans and later started its own production. After the merger the new company was introduced on the stock market and a Finnish competitor bought all the shares. The market for caravans produced in Sweden has always been very nationally oriented. The company is well established in Norway and Finland, but only in exceptional cases is there any export activity outside the Nordic countries. The technology of the product and the methods of caravan production are common knowledge; hence the process of merging the Polar and Sävsjö companies went very smoothly as did the Finnish acquisition. It was after the take-over that the employees observed that Finnish companies can be more hierarchical – that the way of working and behaving is based on a more formalistic concept than Swedish business.

OMP-Konepaja Oy, founded in the 1960s, builds heavy industrial constructions such as weir plants, power stations, and facilities for the forest industry. The company was founded by a large Finnish engineering company, but after a crisis in the middle of the 1980s, OMP was taken over by local private owners and today has approximately 50 employees. Their technology for heavy metal construction is very demanding in terms of resources and time. Most of the activities are executed in the form of projects in very close contact with the customers. One-third of the turnover comes from regional orders in the northern part of Finland. The very small number of potential customers demands a widespread geographical market. The dependence on business cycles and infrastructural investments are obvious and OMP tries to cover the Nordic countries with products and services. The cultural variable is most apparent when doing business with the Russians. Canada is also mentioned; there the employees demand direct instructions instead of the Nordic concept of governing via goals. OMP works very closely with large companies and has observed numerous cultural differences between the two categories of organizations.

In sum, the three conventional companies belong to rather different types of industry but with regard to the basic concept, i.e. traditional manufacturing companies with emphasis on engineering, they are quite similar. The organization of the companies is also typical of manufacturing companies with formal hierarchical levels and departments. Management in these small or medium-sized companies comprises the owner-family or a smaller group of individuals. The companies have been exporting for many decades albeit selling only 5 per cent to 30 per cent of the turnover to foreign countries and with substantial concentration on the neighbouring Nordic countries. It is

Table 2.2 Three case studies – innovative companies

	Norway	Sweden	Finland
Name	Susar AS	Polaris AB	Polar Electro Oy
Industry	Radar-technology – knowledge and systems	Spectacles – design, production, sales	Electronics-recreation sector – R&D, production, marketing
Location	Oslo-science park	North of Sweden – coast town, large public sector	North of Finland – middle-sized town, university and forest industry
Employees	8	50	180
Exports	95%	90%	95%
Export channels	Personal networks	Sales offices and franchising	Sales offices

quite obvious that there are no visible country differences among the three firms studied.

Susar AS, developed in the middle of the 1980s as a spin-off from a government-financed Norwegian research organization in the field of radar technology. The business idea is to serve as an intermediary between the research community and potential end users. The majority of the employees, eight in all, come from various research organizations. Susar reports more than 95 per cent exports. Projects are often very far-reaching in terms of resources and time; the customers are frequently multinationals, military or public companies. Cultural aspects do not affect the professional dimension. The same language with regard to the products and the technology is used world-wide. As a mediator in an advanced technological field, all parties involved need extensive international links. That this industry has relatively few actors underlines the need for a global network.

Polaris AB, is a family business started at the end of the 1970s by the present owner-manager. Their business idea is to design and produce frames for spectacles. Fast growth characterized the first 10 years, but a recent crisis has reduced the number of employees from 160 to 60. In the initial phase a number of production and marketing companies were established in the USA and Germany and later also in Japan and Australia. All of these units are wholly-owned subsidiaries but the current strategy is to convert them into either joint-venture or franchise units. The dominant owner-manager reacts negatively to the domestic cultural difficulties, such as bureaucracy, and feels that it is more difficult to establish a company in Sweden than in Japan. He also favours Japan as a country, which has led to the adoption of a number of Japanese management principles. While the spectacle industry is global in that the companies have to follow and constantly learn and develop new technology in the field of optics, this frame industry is heavily influenced by the fashion industry.

Polar Electro Oy, is a fast-growing company producing electrical equipment – mainly portable heart-rate monitors – for the health, recreation, and sports sector. After 15 years the company employs 180 people, 75 in Finland, 65 in Hong Kong, 30 in the United States, and 10 in Germany. The headquarters is located in a science park near a technical university in Finland, and the founder of the company also works at the university. The main centre outside the home country is in the United States. The health and fitness segments of this market are growing in North America, and it is important to follow technological innovations. The company defines its products as very international. They are promoted via the elite group of athletes and the sales organization is based on customer groups. Only a small part of the turnover comes from domestic sales and very little is sold in the other Nordic countries. The personnel at Polar Electro have not found any reason to reflect on cultural differences within the Nordic countries. Heart-rate monitors are global products, and the markets in Sweden and Norway are very small in an international setting.

In sum, the innovative companies belong to three very different industries; radar technology, spectacles, and electronics. Well-developed links exist with knowledge-intensive organizations, and a highly educated staff manages important projects within R&D, production and marketing. The export share of turnover is very high, and the markets cover all the stronger economic areas of the world. We did not find any country differences in this group.

A MULTILEVEL ANALYSIS

In many respects small firms are linked with the environment – as subcontractors to larger companies or woven into a tight network in a specific industry. Small companies are usually also dependent on certain individuals – the owner-manager or other significant actors – and have limited resources concerning R&D, production or marketing. A situation of multidependence seems obvious for the small firm, which further underlines the importance of using a multilevel approach when studying this category of company.

Nation – the country of the small firm

One of the most evident findings is the absence of difference that can be attributed to country of origin. The companies are situated in three Nordic countries. Trade among these countries is common, and there is a tradition of cooperation, even if there are barriers, such as different languages, between Norway and Finland. We know that the Nordic countries are sometimes described as similar (Haahti 1993), but there are some differences (Hofstede 1980). From the cases it is evident that the companies, whether within the conventional or the innovative group, do not differ across countries. There seems to be a sort of logic that is related more to the companies' operations as such than to country of origin. The role of national culture, for strategic management in internationalization processes at least, seems thus to be quite small. Other influences, such as characteristics of specific industries, are of greater interest. At the same time it is important to bear in mind that this may not apply to large companies;

this could be a trait of small business where the process is strongly linked to individuals rather than to formal structures. That is, it might be that the entrepreneurial way of life takes precedence over national culture in small firms (Höjrup 1983).

Industry – to follow the rules or to create them

All three conventional firms belong to the mechanical-engineering industry. Even if caravans and equipment for offshore or forest industries are different products in terms of production technology, materials etc. the underlying concept follows the same rules. Expensive investments in engineering workshops and an effective organization are central in the general strategy. The main body of employees, blue-collar workers, is focused on portions of the workflow and on improvements in the mechanical equipment. This is also the case for others involved as the owners, the management and the office staff. Although resistance to radically new products, methods and business ideas seems to be very strong, efficiency of production-oriented operations is constantly being improved. This production orientation in the day-to-day business activities and mental map of the management team forms the basis of the underlying rules of the game in these industries.

It is hard to find any greater correspondence to such explicit rules among the three innovative firms. The two firms producing physical goods – portable heart-rate monitors and spectacle frames – have a production based on techniques involving precision tools and electronics. The equipment in production is relatively easy to move. Even though the main part has been retained at the headquarters in the home countries, over the years these two companies have changed their production-plant location a number of times. Moving plants to Asia has reduced the cost of production considerably. As the mediator of radar products between the research community and the end-users, Susar AS is not a player in any specific industrial game. Indirectly though, the rules of the customers, such as the military sector and the ship-yard industry, do set certain limits on their conduct.

It also becomes evident that the basic concept of technology has a different meaning in the two categories of industry. The conventional manufacturing companies rest on an old and established type of technology whereby it is possible to purchase modern production machinery and advanced expertise via well-known market channels. A striking contrast is the process in the innovative companies of developing new types of product or playing the intermediary role between the research community and the commercial end users. This process demands close contacts with organizations and companies close to the technological core of the industry. This continuous search for new commercial breakthroughs, for new products and partners, is a transnational process characterized by giant and rapid steps between countries and continents.

Company – industrial system or narrow product scope

At first glance a caravan seems to be a very specific and clearly defined product, but the involvement of activities in such areas as carriage work, interior design, heating, and motor operations covers a very diverse spectrum and demands heavy investment in specialist staff and separate factory premises. Furthermore, products like caravans are expensive capital goods that demand far-reaching investment in the market organization for retail dealers, customer finance assistance, service, etc. Also the other conventional companies present a complex situation with the role of manufacturer of both products and services or of subcontractor to large firms. In this way these companies are incorporated into a multidimensional industrial system of suppliers, competitors, and other companies. Accordingly individual actors in these industries are constrained by the rules dictated by these networks.

The innovative companies producing heart-rate monitors and frames for spectacles have a very concentrated and well-defined product scope, in which changes over the years can accommodate new designs, colours, and materials. Radar technology is also a specialized area of knowledge and competence. Such a limited product scope implies that it is relatively easy to gain efficiency in all the functions involved in the value-added chain. In all three innovative companies, R&D, the flow and organization of the production, marketing activities, etc. are separate functions with separate personnel, management, and equipment. It is obvious that this clear distinction between the functions has been an advantage in the process of internationalization. During a short period of time, production has been moved between countries and continents in order to find the best possible efficiency. R&D activities are often linked with key strategic individuals somewhere in the world, and the management teams of the home base gain experience from the various markets and countries.

Individual – family and/or profession

The management teams in the conventional companies have characteristics typical of small and medium-sized family-controlled companies, i.e. the owners are very much at the centre of activities and only a few key individuals outside that group are involved in management. The board of directors is solely a formal institution. The only external influence comes from a few people who constitute the small personal networks of the owner-managers. The observation on the industry level that there are some very rigid rules of the game is also evident here; the significant people always act within a narrow band of action. One of the innovative companies, Polaris, is managed as a typical family business. The president of the company exercises his leadership in a rather authoritarian way. Nevertheless, the management of this and of the other two companies has a very open attitude toward the external environment. There are external professional members on the boards, links to universities and research parks are obvious and project groups with hired top-level experts are common.

As far as education is concerned, the mechanical engineering work in the conventional companies demands personnel with a basic education in the field, but the main qualifications come from work experience. The average level of education both for management and on the shop floor is considerably below that of the innovative companies. Polar Electro was founded in a science park by a professor, and the majority of the management team, as well as the white-collar workers in R&D and marketing, have academic backgrounds. Susar's managing director is a former director and coordinator of one of the national research funds in Norway, and the staff of the company consists of top researchers in the field.

This analysis, based directly on the cases, shows that a multilevel approach is essential for an understanding of the internationalization process of small firms. We also found, somewhat to our surprise, that the impact of national aspects was low.

The conventional company from Norway could just as easily have been located in Sweden or Finland or vice versa. The same goes for the innovative companies. The way of reasoning and description of the internationalization processes cannot be said to differ at all among these countries, at least not in these types of company. We will, therefore, not elaborate any further on the issue of national culture in the remainder of our paper; we end this discussion by referring instead to Postman's (1993) thesis that technology has taken precedence over social culture in our modern world – which may explain why there are no national differences while there are differences between types of industry.

In the concluding section we will discuss the three levels – industry, company, and individual – to contribute to a deeper understanding of the dynamics shaping the internationalization processes in the companies studied.

DISCUSSION AND CONCLUSION

In the literature, the structure and dynamics of industries within a nation or a region are often studied in terms of business systems. Such systems are shaped by a set of contextual factors common for a sector or group of companies. The business-system notion is used in attempts to explain the behaviour of individual companies or when making analyses of industries (Whitley 1992; Sölvell *et al.* 1991). The three conventional companies in this study rest on a production-oriented culture. The technological concept focuses on manufacturing, and the companies are woven into a system of large companies, sub-contractors, and customers. We find it appropriate to extend the discussion about industrial wisdom (Spender 1989; Hellgren and Melin 1992), valid for the specified industries and business sectors, to the basic structures in manufacturing environments. Distinctive traits of all three companies are: technological focus on traditional manufacturing issues; well-defined roles in a market hierarchy; and R&D activities based on gradual improvements to established products and routines rather than the creation of entirely new types of products. Concentration on local (Kristiansands Skruefabrik), national, or Nordic markets (Polar & Sävsjö and OMP) defines the natural task environments for the companies and the industries they are a part of.

One explanation for the global view of the innovative companies is their narrow product scope. It is relatively easy to deconstruct business activities in research and development, production, marketing, etc. and to find an effective way of organizing and executing these functions on an international basis.

Business systems here are loose couplings between free-standing actors or a network with only a limited number of actors. Other studies indicate that an advanced technological level combined with shorter product life cycles drive companies to invest more intensively in the internationalization process in order to achieve the necessary market volume within a limited time span. Whereas this partially confirms our results, the situation will be even more accentuated for companies coming from small countries with a small home market.

The two categories of company in this study also reveal differences in company culture and management style. As we have seen, the conventional companies are deeply rooted in specific markets within which movements to improve products, learn customer preferences or

exploit new niches are made stepwise. The management contribution
to strategies is at an administrative level. The vital routines for bud-
geting, sales planning, and investment policies are executed by special
personnel using special routines. The innovative companies are characterized by an entrepreneurial culture and a strategic management to
a great extent of a tentative nature. The narrow product scope and
well-defined demarcation between R&D, production and marketing
seems to facilitate an organization that can effectively execute the
various ongoing projects. However, the real strategies are a result of
a continuous flow of new opportunities and short-term goals. In
Mintzberg's (1989) terminology, this would be strategy as a pattern
in a stream of actions. Often the strategies are linked to the functional
areas within the company. All three companies have thus far been
successful in coordinating this broad mapping of activities and trans-
ferring these activities to profitable operations.

In the conventional companies, a handful of significant actors both
initiate and are involved in the execution of decisions. The main body
in these groups comprises members of the controlling family or the
equivalent clan of old friends. The individuals in the innovative companies have a very high educational level and execute single projects in
a dedicated and unbureaucratic order. They vary from teams with
partners in other companies, in research institutions, and even jointly
with competitors. Professionalism within the companies and in the
way they build and maintain external networks is high.

The distinctive features of the companies studied have been related
to three levels: industry, company, and individual. We have found that
the internationalization process in conventional companies is very
dependent on, or even fettered to, the structure of the industry and
management by a rigid administrative type of company culture. The
inner circle of close relatives or friends dominates the organization.
The innovative companies, on the other hand, are relatively free from
industrial structures, and have an entrepreneurial culture with strategies for quick action. They also have substantial elements of professionalism. These findings are summarized in Table 2.3.

The process through which a company becomes internationally
oriented depends not only on a change of perspective – from domestic
or local to international. Even if important functions are transferred
abroad or added to the company, the need for a home base is still there,
and sometimes it becomes even more important. This is a situation
confronting the internationally active company. A comprehensive body
of research has discussed theories and practical solutions for achieving
a balance between global strategies and local attachment (Doz 1986).

Table 2.3 Conventional and innovative companies – main characteristics

	Convention companies	Innovative companies
Level		
Industry	Industrial wisdom	Industrial ignorance
Company	Administrative culture	Mapping culture
Individual	Family/clan	Professionalism
International focus	Local	Global

Single firms must constantly review the effects of being more global or more local in their international operations. The term localize suggests the vast number of dimensions that can be focused in analysing the scale ranging from local to global or vice versa. These aspects can be understood in terms of centralization-decentralization, global-local leadership, and strategies-control (Gustavsson, *et al.* 1993; Bengtsson and Bonnedahl 1993).

For the conventional companies, the common denominator will be the local focus. The reason for international activities can often be found in incidental causes or because over-capacity has forced the company abroad. The concept of psychic distance is relevant and is seen in the stepwise behaviour, e.g. when companies start selling to neighbouring countries first and gradually go on selling to more distant markets. The constant need for new types of products is not obvious in these industries. Instead the norm for the industry requires well-defined restricted roles for the participants. The individuals have a strong commitment to the region, the industry, the company, and the family and therefore see many of the international activities as necessary evil.

The common denominator for the innovative companies is the global focus. These companies work in a proactive way where the technology built into the products invigorates the companies so that they make international moves (Simon 1992). The products can be a new concept (heart-rate monitors or technological solutions in the radar business) or linked to the short life cycle of fashion products (spectacles). The significant actors are relatively numerous, all with a distinct international scope in terms of education, experience, interest, and ambition. The international concept will be that fast-growing companies acquire new units instead of building step-wise and that strategic core investments are made in expensive software networking, prototypes and marketing, rather than in physical goods.

To summarize our conclusions, we found two distinct forms of processes for internationalization: the innovative companies' global focus and the traditional companies' local focus. Another way of putting this is to state that innovative companies are free to follow whatever route they wish, except for the imperative that stems from the technology chosen. They may structure business activities, company forms and other functions quite freely. The innovative companies in our cases are both of a high tech and a less advanced nature. This does not seem to have any effect, i.e. the level of technology does not seem to be the important thing. The newness of the technology seems to be the relevant indicator for how free the process may be *vis-à-vis* the industrial wisdom. So the technological imperative is essential, not on the basis of its level alone but due more to the freedom generated by new technology.

Of course the technological imperative is inherent and extremely important even in traditional business, but here the technological factor has become intertwined with other factors in the organization and in the industry to such an extent that it is impossible to separate the different factors. This does not mean that technology is not important, as is actually shown by our cases, where the industry *per se* seems to be much more important than country of origin for explaining the internationalization process. This dominance of industry characteristics is indicated by Chatman and Jehn (1994), who in their study found that industry characteristics overruled organizational cultures – or rather found that the industry formed the organizational culture.

We referred earlier to Postman (1993) and his analysis of the technological influence in our society. It seems that our study confirms the importance of technology in forming the cultural norms and values in business. This is even more accentuated in those cases where we have innovative technology, i.e. where we have a situation with few structural rules. Then the technology determines the routes taken and does so quite effectively. In time, new patterns of industrial wisdom will emerge from the newcomers. Again we would also like to point out that it is not the technology as such that determines whether new industrial sectors will emerge; rather it is the innovative element – the newness – that makes this possible.

Naturally, it is also important to note that there are forces on a higher level that limit the forms of emerging industrial sectors. One such force is the internationalization process in the Western world. Today, inasmuch as all business companies are well aware of the global market, this global outlook exists in the minds of people.

Another force that homogenizes the forms of new sectors is the development of communications. All companies today have access to global communications networks, if they wish. Such forces, together with the wisdom of existing industrial sectors, make it more natural for new sectors to have a global outlook. This in turn might create problems in the local settings in the future – if the industrial sector is defined strictly for a global purpose.

To sum up, we have discussed the specific settings concerning values, norms, languages, etc. in different countries. Our cases have shown that the factors that we initially thought were of ultimate importance when studying the internationalization process in companies lack relevance. Instead we conclude that the concept of industry, combined with studies on company and individual level, capture the essence of internationalization processes in small firms.

APPENDIX

Research method – conduct of interviews and interpretation of data

This study was conducted by case studies in two different types of companies in Norway, Sweden and Finland (six companies in all). To get reliable and valid data we started by selecting companies through a process where we formed a list of companies based on our earlier studies and on information from colleagues in Norway and Finland. We also contacted business organizations. After that we selected companies that were obviously conventional and innovative respectively. We got ready access to all the companies.

As the companies are small (one has only eight employees, four range between 47 and 80, and one has 180 employees) strategic management is handled by top management. This means that we contacted the CEO with our questions. The CEO is also our chosen respondent. The exception is the largest company where after initial contact with the CEO, we met the manager who, through delegation, had the responsibility for strategic issues for the internationalization process. In each company, we consequently interviewed the person responsible for internationalization. In all companies this person is solely responsible for internationalization, and in most cases has been so since the company started. The first interview lasted between three and four hours and at that time we also asked to be shown around the premises. This was not a problem, as all the companies are fairly small in production and administration. The interviews were taped, with permission from all respondents.

Our interviews confirmed that our respondents were all clearly responsible for internationalization in their companies, which means that information was given from the person in charge of strategies in international affairs. Because our interviews were taped, there was little danger of distortion. It was also an advantage that the two of us made all interviews together since that meant that we could follow up answers better and our interpretations could be validated against each other's.

Since we followed our scheme of questions (described below), we had the opportunity to check for missing information and follow up questions substantially during the first interview. Afterwards we made verbatim transcriptions of the interviews. Then we posted these to the respondents and asked for their comments. At the same time we phoned them to fill in the few gaps that we found in our material. We also used other indirect information on the companies and on the leadership style. We searched for literature: articles; company information in annual reports; and earlier research on the chosen companies. In one case we had conducted research on the company a few years before this study and in another we could make use of the material that a colleague had access to. This type of information was mostly used for validation purposes.

The interview aimed at finding out what the internationalization process looked like in the companies (specifically looking for country differences). The same questions were asked in all the companies, even if the ordering of them differed slightly due to the respondents' way of answering. The interviews may be described as semi-structured, where we had a list of questions we wanted answered but where we let the respondent's line of reasoning form the structure of the interview.

We had arranged beforehand the questions to follow, the type of logic that in our experience functions most efficiently when interviewing small business managers. This meant that we started with general questions about the manager and his role in the company and then went on to general questions about the company. Since these companies are all small, there is a strong interdependence between the history and description of the individual and the company. After the more descriptive and broad questions we went on to questions on internationalization behaviour. Here we focused on how the companies acted in this arena and how the manager viewed internationalization in the wider context of the company as a whole. We specifically asked about views on cultural differences. Finally, we asked questions about the manager's view on the conditions and the internationalization logic of the industry to which the company belonged. During the interviews, we posed the questions in the same manner where we took the initiative, and when the respondents touched upon one of our questions before we had posed it, we used our questions in its original form as a controlling question.

Since this is an exploratory study, the data from the six cases are quite manageable. When we prepared for the typed transcripts of the interviews to be sent to the respondents, it was already obvious to us that the companies represented different categories, not based on the national background. After we got permission to use the transcripts, we first analysed the material to describe the characteristics of the companies (see Tables 2.1 and 2.2). Here we put together the main characteristics of each company with regard to location, type of industry, number of employees, exports and export channels. Other descriptions were included at first (as turnover), but during the analysis we reduced the information to the things most important to our basic question.

The next step in the analysis was to find out if there were any differences between the companies concerning the internationalization processes. Here we used the respondents' descriptions of how internationalization comes about at an individual, company and industry level, respectively. Our original thought that national differences would exist was not supported; instead, there was a striking similarity among the three companies in each category – conventional and innovative. This clustering around category of industry rather than by country, size or other factors permeates all levels. The short case descriptions included in the article aim at giving this overall impression of the companies in the two categories, almost divided by a demarcation line. These descriptions were also sent to the companies so that we could have permission to publish our results without the necessity of anonymity.

To code and interpret the data both of us started working individually on the interview material in raw form. Then we discussed our categories and worked together to form the constructs in terms of the levels (industry, company and individual) that we found different between the companies. We also checked for alternative interpretations that focused on size and nation as distinguishing factors, but the results showed that the category of industry was the deciding factor in terms of internationalization behaviour.

NOTES

1 Reprinted by permission of the publisher from *Journal of Business Venturing*, vol. 11, no. 6, November 1996, pp. 471–87. Copyright 1 by Elsevier Science Inc.

REFERENCES

Adler N.J. (1986) *International Dimensions of Organizational Behaviour*, Boston, MA: Kent.

Aharoni, Y. (1966) *The Foreign Investment Decision Process*, Cambridge, MA: Harvard University Press.

Andersson, S. and Lundin, A.R. (1992) 'Internationalisering av mindre företag – En övning i småskaligt nätverksbyggande', in C. Fredriksson (ed.) *Glokalisering – Om konsten att tänkä globalt och handla localt* (Glocalizing – To think globally and act locally), Umeå, Sweden: Umeå Business School, pp. 111–24.

Ansoff, H.I. (1979) 'Aspirations and culture in strategic behaviour', Working Paper No. 79–12, Brussels: European Institute for Advanced Studies in Management.

Bartlett, C.A. and Ghoshal, S. (1989) *Managing Across Borders: The Transnational Solution*. Cambridge, MA: Harvard Business School Press.

Bartlett, C.A. and Ghoshal, S. (1991) 'Global strategic management: Impact on the new frontiers of strategy research', *Strategic Management Journal*, 12 Special Issue – Summer: 5–16.

Bengtsson, M. and Bonnedahl, K.J. (1993) 'European integration and strategy – Implications for the manufacturing SME – Towards local or global niche-seeking', paper presented at 23rd European Small Business Seminar, Belfast, N. Ireland.

Bilkey, W.J. and Tesar, G. (1977) 'The export behaviour of smaller sized Wisconsin manufacturing firms', *Journal of International Business Studies*, 8:33–46.

Boter, H. and Holmquist, C. (1994) 'Internationalization of small and medium-sized industries in manufacturing', *Interstratos,* Version 4: 1991–1992–1993–1994. Umeå, Sweden: Umeå Business School.

Calori, R. and de Woot, P. (eds) (1994) *A European Management Model. Beyond Diversity*, London: Prentice Hall.

Cavusgil, S.T. (1980) 'On the internationalization process of firms', *European Research,* November, 8 (6):273–81.

Chatman, J.A. and Jehn, K.A. (1994) 'Assessing the relationship between industry characteristics and organizational culture: How different can you be?', *Academy of Management Journal*, 37:522–53.

Child, J. (1988) 'On organization in their sectors', *Organizational Studies,* 9:13–19.

Deal, T. and Kennedy, A. (1982) *Corporate Cultures*. Reading, MA: Addison Wesley.

Doz, Y. (1986) *Strategic Management in Multinational Companies*, Oxford: Pergamon Press.

Frost, P.J., Moore, L.F., Louis, M.R., Lundberg, C.C. and Martin, J. (1985) *Organizational Culture*, London: Sage.

Gandemo, B. and Andersson, T.D. (1993) *When Small Firms Go International*, Gothenburg, Sweden: Gothenburg School of Economics.

Gustavsson, P., Melin, L. and MacDonald, S. (1993) 'Learning to glocalise', paper presented at the workshop on Organizational Capabilities and Internationalization Processes, Paris, Ecole Superieur des Sciences Economiques Commerciales.

Haahti, A.J. (ed.) (1993) 'Interstratos – Internationalization of Strategic Orientations of European Small and Medium-Sized Enterprises', *EIASM Working Papers,* 1–93, Brussels.

Hedlund, G. and Kverneland, A. (1984) *Investing in Japan – The Experience of Swedish Firms,* Stockholm, Sweden: Institute of International Business, Stockholm School of Economics.

Hellgren, B. and Melin, L. (1992) 'Business systems, industrial wisdom and corporate strategies', in R. Whitley (ed.), *European Business Systems. Firms and Markets in Their National Contexts,* London: Sage, pp. 180–97.

Hickson, D. and MacMillan, C.J. (eds) (1981) *Organization and Nation,* Farnborough, England: Gower.

Hofstede, G. (1980) *Culture's Consequences,* London: Sage.

Höjrup, T. (1983) *Det Glemte Folk: Livsformer og Centraldirigering. (The Forgotten People: Lifestyles and Centralized Control),* Hörsholm, Denmark: Statens byggeforskninginstitut.

Jahoda, G. (1992) *Crossroads between Culture and Mind: Continuities and Change in Theories of Human Nature,* London: Harvester-Wheatsheaf.

Johanson, J., and Mattson, L.G. (1988) 'Internationalization in industrial systems – a network approach', in N. Hood and J.E. Vahlne (eds.) *Strategies in Global Competition,* New York: Croom Helm, pp. 287–314.

Johanson, J. and Vahlne, J.E. (1977) 'The internationalization process in the firm – a model of knowledge development and increasing market commitments', *Journal of International Business Studies,* 8, Spring-Summer: 23–32.

Johanson, J. and Wiedersheim-Paul, F. (1975) 'The internationalization of the firm – four Swedish cases', *Journal of Management Studies,* 12 (3): 305–22.

Klofsten, M. (1992) *Tidiga utvecklingsprocesser i teknikbaserade företag. (Early stages of development in small high tech firms),* Dissertation: University of Linköping.

Kornadt, H.J., Eckensberger, L.H. and Emminghaus, W.B. (1980) 'Cross-cultural research on motivation and its contribution to a general theory of motivation', in H.C. Triadis and W. Lonner (eds) *Handbook of Cross-Cultural Psychology. Basic Processes,* vol. 3, Boston, MA: Allyn and Bacon, pp. 223–321.

Lindqvist, M. (1991) *Infant Multinationals – The Internationalization of Young, Technology-based Swedish Firms,* Dissertation: Institute of International Business, Stockholm School of Economics.

Lyles, M.A. (1990) 'A research agenda for strategic management in the 1990s', *Journal of Management Studies,* 27, (4): 363–75.

Melin, L. (1992) 'Internationalization as a strategy process', *Strategic Management Journal,* 13 Special Issue – Winter: 99–118.

Mintzberg, H. (1989) *Mintzberg on Management. Inside Our Strange World of Organizations,* New York: The Free Press.

Nilsson, K. and Nilsson, P. (1992) *Småföretag i flerpartssamverkan – En studie av aktörer, byggstenar och fogmassa vid nätverksbyggande (Multibusiness Cooperation Systems – A Study of Actors, Bricks and Concrete in the Construction of Networks Between Small Enterprises),* Dissertation: Umeå Business School.

Nordström, K.A. (1991) *The Internationalization Process of the Firm – Searching For New Patterns and Explanations,* Dissertation: Institute for International Business, Stockholm School of Economics.

Porter, M.E. (ed.) (1986) *Competition in Global Industries*, Boston, MA: Harvard Business School Press.

Porter, M.E. (1990) *The Competitive Advantage of Nations*, New York: The Free Press.

Postman, N. (1993) *Technopoly. The Surrender of Culture to Technology*, New York: Vintage Books.

Prahalad, C.K. and Doz, Y. (1987) *The Multinational Mission*, New York: The Free Press.

Sharma, D. (1991) *International Operations of Professional Firms*, Lund, Sweden: Studentlitteratur.

Simon, H. (1992) 'Lessons from Germany's midsize giants', *Harvard Business Review*, 70 (March-April): 116–23.

Sölvell, O., Zander, I. and Porter, M.E. (1991) *Advantage Sweden*, Stockholm, Sweden: Norstedts.

Spender, J.C. (1989) *Industry Recipes. An Enquiry into the Nature and Sources of Management Judgement*, Oxford: Basil Blackwell.

Stymne, B. (1970) *Values and Processes. A Systems Study of Effectiveness in Three Organizations*, Dissertation: Lund University.

Tayed, M. (1988) *Organizations and National Culture*, London: Sage.

Turner, B.A. (1971) *Exploring the Industrial Sub-culture*, London: Macmillan.

Whitley, R. (ed.) (1992) *European Business Systems: Firms and Markets in Their National Contexts*, London: Sage.

3 Forms and extent of success factors

The case of Switzerland

Hans J. Pleitner, Jürgen Brunner and Margrit Habersaat

INTRODUCTION

Companies that seek to gain or retain international competitiveness in the world-wide process of integration have to develop success factors to stand out from their national and international competitors. This task becomes a gigantic challenge for every company, particularly considering the new economic macro constellation (integration of the European Union [EU] and the metamorphosis of GATT to the World Trade Organisation [WTO]).

Whereas the big companies – at least seemingly – are dealing calmly with the new situation (Wüthrich and Winter 1994: 305), the small and medium-sized enterprises (SMEs) find themselves confronted with the need for reconsidering and examining their strategies and strategic alternatives, insofar as they do have a strategy at all. In either case, this need for a strategy certainly now arises.

For the Swiss SMEs the case is even more delicate, considering their position outside the EU – unless, of course, they decide to re-focus their business activities to geographical areas outside the EU.[1] The intent of this paper is to outline the factors and conditions that help Swiss companies succeed in the process of internationalization, as compared to other European companies.[2]

THE SWISS SITUATION

The economic framework of today is characterized by the increasing internationalization extending to globalization, frequent economic up and down-turns, an increasing speed of technological development and a societal change in values extending into other dimensions of economic activities as well.

However, we consider the global process of integration to be the main challenge for all enterprises. This liberalization quest and the concrete reduction of trade and investment barriers leads – despite all resistance and 'counter-liberalization' movements – to the formation of common economic areas in the various regions of this ever more integrating globe.

This process itself evokes the clashing of the various cultures, which – contrary to some experiences incurred at the political level – can be economically integrated and actually may lead to changed ways of thinking and doing business – assuming, of course, that the 'superior' culture does not supersede the other culture(s).

As a third alternative, we may find the creation of a multi-cultural area, exemplified by Switzerland. In the Swiss case we find the varieties and even differences of the various languages and cultures to be in tune and – maybe even as consequence – to have reached political and economic stability. Building on this stability as well as on a heavily diversified and ever internationally oriented economy, we find Switzerland to have attained high quality standards and a remarkable ability to innovate in a competitive environment. The economic efficiency and output of Switzerland is ranked high among the industrialized nations, in the categories of worker productivity and gross domestic product (GDP) per capita, which can be attributed to the large inflows of foreign capital and the subsequent investment activity. This rank however is jeopardized by for example such factors as increasing labour cost (Borner *et al.* 1991: 36, 91).

The role of the SMEs in this positive development is significant. SMEs act as stabilisers in times of economic up and down-turns, contribute to a stable employment situation and assure a regionally balanced economic structure (Bundesminister 1989: 128 and 1991: 135). A necessary condition however, for the continuing growth of the Swiss economy is – as was stressed earlier – the existence of internationally competitive companies, and in particular SMEs.

Switzerland has a long tradition of foreign trade, especially with the European countries. With the creation of the European Union, Switzerland is faced with a new framework (Pleitner and Müller 1990: 226, 232). Up to now Switzerland was granted access to national markets, even as a non-EU member, due to free trade agreements. This domain of free trade outside the EU-boundaries is predetermined to decrease and subsequently will bring competitive disadvantages for the Swiss. It is not assumed that Switzerland will be totally excluded. However its foreign trade with the EU will become increasingly difficult and thus will remain dependent upon bilateral concessions granted unwillingly from the EU.

At the present time Switzerland remains an important trade partner with the EU; however its significance has been decreasing due to the increasing trade within the EU. The trading with Switzerland now accounts for a mere 4 percent of the total volume of EU trade, meanwhile 75 percent of the Swiss imports still originate from the EU and 56 percent of the Swiss exports are being sold to the EU (Neue Zürcher Zeitung 1995: 27).

The increasing trade within the EU (9 per cent growth in 1994), accentuated through the recent expansion of the EU, will however diminish the weight of the Swiss foreign trade with the EU. Because of that fact, countries outside the EU and the WTO as a whole, will become increasingly significant for Switzerland. A trend can be detected towards increased foreign trade with the OECD countries and the Pacific Rim, as well as with the developing South American countries and the countries of Eastern Europe.

The enhancement of foreign trade with South Korea, Taiwan and mainland China, though, signifies new risks for the home market. The expected competitive pressure through decreasing prices (especially through lower labour costs), an increasing product quality and swelling product offerings, mean a qualified challenge for the Swiss companies. Albeit that Switzerland represents an attractive and internationally competitive location, it is massively threatened. To confront and defy this threat companies need to strategically reposition themselves, anticipating market developments and revitalizing the economic efficiency and output (increased productivity, cost reductions, ever increased ability to innovate). Only with the successful management of the above challenges, can a competitive advantage be gained in this new situation (Bamberger and Pleitner 1988: 83).

This challenge applies to SMEs as well as to large corporations. Many times in the past SMEs were faced with stiff competition, which 'educated' them to allocate their resources efficiently, be active innovators and become quick in adapting.

Henceforth, Swiss companies need not be afraid about the recent developments. However, they must prepare themselves well for this increased market competition. The necessary conditions for the process of the internationalization of the Swiss SMEs seem to be in place. The degree to which this process of internationalization has been attained is to be considered in the following section.

FORMS OF INTERNATIONALIZATION

Internationalization as a gradual process

In light of the projected developments at the international level, many SMEs started early on to integrate foreign business activities into their strategic plans (Pleitner 1985: 150ff). Since that planning stage the actual internationalization process has evolved through several stages. These stages or phases can be interpreted as moving with increased intensity towards international business activities and are accompanied by remarkable adaptation as well as innovation (Johanson and Wiederheim 1975: 306; Steinmann *et al.* 1981: 108). This internationalization process has – at every stage – two dimensions, which are the input of management activity and the input of capital. By that we mean the amount of capital invested, the degree of autonomy of the foreign subsidiary, and the way and extent to which resources are transferred abroad.

The chosen dimensions of capital and management activity determine – as can be seen in Figure 3.1 – the degree of international

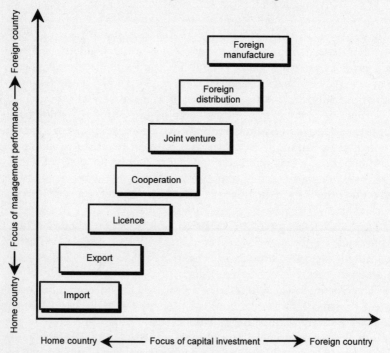

Figure 3.1 Dimensions of the process of internationalization
Source: Based on Meissner/Gerber 1980: 224

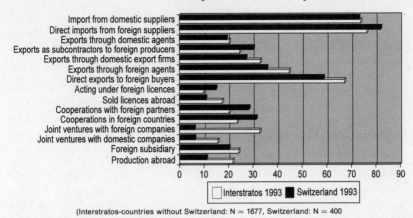

(Interstratos-countries without Switzerland: N = 1677, Switzerland: N = 400

Figure 3.2 Activities in foreign countries

involvement, ranging from mere import/export to foreign production sites. If one now examines the utilization of the various possible choices by SMEs (see Figure 3.2), we find that export and import (in its direct form) prevail within the SMEs of Western Europe; however, greater differences can be observed if comparing different scenarios among countries. The Swiss SMEs, for example, do tend to engage in international cooperation agreements more than other countries.[3]

Scenarios with low capital and management activity

Usually, the first step taken by SMEs in the process of internationalization is the import of foreign goods. In this scenario the companies continue to sell their products in the home market. However, they receive their supplies from abroad. These supplies are purchased either directly from the foreign supplier (82 per cent in the case of the Swiss SMEs) or are bought through domestic agents (73 per cent). Currently, over 40 per cent of the SMEs' supplies are purchased from a foreign supplier, which can be considered a major impact.

Exports, defined as the delivery of goods or services abroad, is also a 'classic' form of business activity of SMEs outside their home market (Mugler and Miesenböck 1990: 1). Here we can also distinguish between a direct and indirect form of export, depending upon whether the company in question directly delivers its goods or services to the foreign customer, or rather it is involving a domestic agent. Direct export signifies the larger part of exports as well with medium-sized enterprises as with the small enterprises (ca. 60 per cent in the Swiss case); only 20–25 per cent of the SMEs chose to export via the involvement of a domestic agent. Albeit the percentage of direct exports of the Swiss SMEs seems impressively high, one must not forget that SMEs in other Western European countries achieve even higher percentages – in spite of the export-oriented image of the Swiss. Are we already witnessing the effects of the European integration on the SMEs of our EU neighbours?

Scenarios with high capital and management activity

The most intensive and complex form foreign orientation can take is direct investment, either by opening an own foreign subsidiary (realised by 20 per cent of Swiss SMEs) or establishing their own foreign production sites (11 per cent). In this scenario as well, we find the Swiss SMEs to be below the Western European average, which might be signalling the SMEs' conflict between image-conforming foreign economic activity and the no less image-conforming economic caution.

This seems to indicate that up to now the Swiss SMEs – if in doubt – rated the risk of financing and venturing into such activity higher than the potential advantages of such stand-alone foreign operation, promising lower costs. Qualitatively speaking, we find the heart of the problem of successful direct foreign investment to lie in the uncertainty of the transferability of known management and company strategies and concepts into the culture of the prospective target country.

Scenarios with medium capital and management activity

The reason for the apparent holding back of the Swiss SMEs as it pertains to joint ventures (6 per cent) and licensing (11 per cent) remains to be answered, but at the same time it seems to indicate the need – or at least the potential – for development. In the case of the low number of Joint Venture engagements, we tend to believe this to be caused by the fear of losing independence. However this risk is less prevalent in the classic cooperation agreements – explaining the above average activity of the Swiss SMEs within this dimension. In the case of licensing, where more licenses are obtained than given, we find it hard to attribute causality. Could this possibly indicate that Swiss SMEs, after all, are less innovative than they were thought to be?

Concerning the different scenarios with extreme variances in the country comparisons, it seems worthwhile to consider the development over time. As to the cross border cooperation agreements, we find the number of cooperating companies to have increased across industries, in some sectors we can even observe a doubling of cooperation agreements over the course of a few years. This was particularly true for the areas of sales (39 per cent), expansion of product offerings (28 per cent), research and development (24 per cent), customer service and market research (both 23 per cent).

Even the least popular case of joint venture, or strategic alliance, is a form of internationalization that has been selected increasingly by the Swiss SMEs over the past few years, particularly since – if the agreement works out – the risk can be shared equally, implying that SMEs can profit from a foreign investment without carrying the risk all by themselves.

INTERNATIONAL ORIENTATION OF SMEs

Market development and competitive positioning

With the global opening of markets, companies are being offered increasing opportunities, though at the cost of intensified competition in the home market. This necessitates of SMEs that their products and services have to become more competitive, thus enabling them to survive. In this changing competitive environment, the process of internationalization becomes the source of realising new opportunities, i.e. providing it plays its part for survival through the utilization of new profit opportunities in new markets via the creation of new value added potentials.

The opportunities for internationalization may be found concretely in the realization of entrepreneurial accomplishments, namely through a more efficient production process, utilization of standardization or differentiation, optimal resource usage, realization of price, cost and time advantages regarding the access of resources, a more optimal capacity use, participation in technology transfer and the attainment of additional management skills and knowledge.

These opportunities for internationalization, of course, are confronted by equally great threats. Activities abroad may mean seemingly insurmountable obstacles for SMEs. These may occur through high information costs, rather long decision making processes caused by the lack of knowledge and experience of the foreign market, new legal and cultural frameworks, market insecurity facilitated by economic instability and exchange rate risks, uncollectables because of unknown payment ethics, transportation costs incurred by central production, tariffs and other trade barriers, costs of organization (planning and coordinating activities) and the possibly higher than usual need for capital (Gaugler and Ganter 1995).

At least subjectively, SMEs seem to have to overcome greater obstacles in this process of internationalization, as compared to their larger competitors. The discovery of foreign niche markets and the utilisation of their SME-specific advantages, may however compensate SMEs for the above mentioned potential disadvantages as compared to the larger corporations. Nevertheless, one must not forget the SME-specific disadvantages as well. See Table 3.1.

The main motives for a positive decision towards international activities are an enlarged market, increased growth, more efficient capacity usage and greater opportunity to market product and services. The above average administrative burden of SMEs engaged in cross border trade, however, remains a key obstacle to their internationalization (Hurni 1995: 129). Another major impediment – considering the export scenario – is the high cost and price structure on the home market. Considered to be of less importance are factors such as low appreciation of entrepreneurs at home, proximity to suppliers and raw material availability (Brunner and Habersaat 1994: 59).

The actual development of international activities is also strongly influenced by the competitive conditions and framework abroad. The analysis of these conditions clearly shows that the pricing situation intensifies and that large and/or foreign companies act to intensify competition. In this study we find at no time any factor showing a decreased competitive intensity. Interestingly, we see Swiss entrepren-

Table 3.1 Strengths and weaknesses of the internationalization of SMEs

Strengths	Weaknesses
• High quality standards and individualized product and service offerings while enjoying a flexible cost structure • Flexibility through concentration of decision making authority and short information structure • Spontaneous ability to adapt to changing market environments and customer needs • Ability to avoid overpowering ideology and bureaucracy through personalized communication.	• Difficulty recruiting qualified employees because of limited possibilities for advancement • Centralization of decision making authority insufficient for an international enterprise • Competitive disadvantages through weak position to negotiate, limited market influence and lack of knowledge of target markets • Shortage of financing opportunities and increased risk potential with small equity basis • Mostly involved with day-to-day activities hardly finding time for strategic management and focus on marketing

eurs ranking the development of factors such as price, quality, technology, foreign competitors, tendencies for cooperation and concentration (signifying the majority of factors!) as more competition-intensifying than do their colleagues from Western Europe.[4] An interpretation of this finding remains difficult. Objectively speaking, one would not expect the development of these factors to be putting the Swiss in a worse position than any other nation participating in this study. This then implies that the above finding might be caused by a more 'realistic', i.e. pessimistic view of the Swiss entrepreneurs, or it might be linked to the perception of being isolated from the EU (of the eight participating nations, only Switzerland and Norway are not EU members). See Figure 3.3.

Intensity of internationalization

Despite the difficulties and impediments portrayed we find more and more Western European SMEs entering foreign markets. Within the overall study, about two thirds of the internationally orientated SMEs are actively and more than one third reactively market-oriented. This orientation was measured through the average number of orders from foreign countries. And if one closely analyses the data, we find the Swiss SMEs to be lagging more than 20 per cent behind all other Western European SMEs.

And again – contrary to the projected image of Switzerland – we can hardly consider the Swiss SMEs to be at the forefront of the

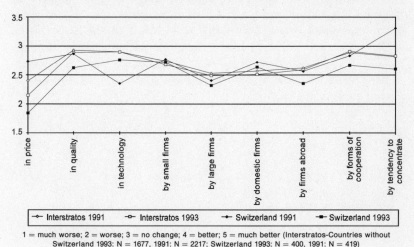

1 = much worse; 2 = worse; 3 = no change; 4 = better; 5 = much better (Interstratos-Countries without Switzerland 1993: N = 1677, 1991: N = 2217; Switzerland 1993: N = 400, 1991: N = 419)

Figure 3.3 Perceived changes in market position

internationalization process. However, the developments within recent years show clearly that they are increasing their international activities and are progressing (Brunner and Habersaat 1994: 67).

The overall increasing intensity of market penetration is also evident from the far larger number of companies starting international activities than those closing down their international activities (in the area of starting exports 40 per cent, starting imports 20 per cent, starting direct investment 6 per cent, whereas the export stopped is 7 per cent, import stopped 8 per cent, and direct investment stopped 2 per cent). This observation is taken as a clear indication of the continual growing international orientation of the Swiss SMEs, showing – as compared to the other European enterprises – the Swiss are catching up. The strategic orientation of the Swiss SMEs is clearly distinguished by a popular combination of various strategies.[5]

These combined internationalization strategies are often carried out with a rather low management and capital intensity. However in the end we can speak of a rather high intensity level: This combination of individually less intensive strategies, compensates for a missing capital and management intensive strategy (e.g. joint venture, direct investment).

These export and import strategies are often combined with each other, and cooperation agreements are carried out by almost every second company in addition, implying after all an export and import engagement.

Even without the aspects of combination, the sheer number of differing internationalizing strategies can be seen as an indicator for the international orientation. Only 11 per cent of the Swiss SMEs operating abroad utilize exclusively one internationalization strategy, whereas 67 per cent utilize three or more strategies. In a wider sense, at most every company is somehow engaged abroad. See Table 3.2.

Table 3.2 Combination of international strategies (% of all companies)

Strategy	Import	Export	Licence	Cooperation	Joint venture	Direct investment
Import		72	20	42	11	24
Export	95		23	45	13	29
Licence	98	83		52	23	35
Cooperation	92	76	24		20	30
Joint venture	95	88	44	84		51
Direct investment	99	92	29	56	23	

INTERNATIONALIZATION AND SUCCESS

Comparison of all success factors

To secure the success of a company it takes the attainment of specific strengths, which enable a company to obtain a competitive advantage, e.g. through better development. These factors for success are thus 'producing' – via the increased competitiveness – the company's success and profitability.

At the empirical analysis of the success factors of SMEs (Figure 3.4) we find a Europe-wide dominance – interestingly enough with little deviance between the participating countries, i.e. between Switzerland and the remaining countries – of product quality, reliability of delivery and flexibility, in addition to factors such as management quality, workers' skills, customer service/relations and local image. These rankings were made by the participating managers.

We conclude from the above results that merely a 'good product' will not guarantee success in the foreign market place, but the interplay of a number of factors will. Interestingly, we find little significance in the price factor, implying that sole niche-marketing and a differentiation strategy may not cause increased competitive pressures – assuming they are placing their product in the higher priced market

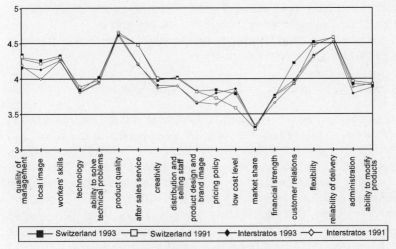

1 = no importance; 2 = low importance; 3 = medium importance; 4 = high importance;
5 = very high importance
(Interstratos-countries without Switzerland 1993: N = 1677, 1991: N = 2217; Switzerland 1993: N = 400, 1991: N = 419)

Figure 3.4 Success factors of internationalization in general

segment. Least significance is found with the market share factor. Thus, apparently companies do not seek to attain competitive advantages through the utilization of a high market share. This is quite a remarkable finding, considering that particularly in the Anglo-Saxon countries a high market share is assumed to be of central importance to the companies' success.[6] We find extended significance attributed to the technology factor and the ability to solve technical problems.

The fact of the rather small deviance of the success factors in this Western European comparison, seems to indicate to us that the results might actually not be too far from reality, considering the answers given stem from practitioners themselves.

Comparison of success factors (according to specific characteristics)

Considering the little deviance we have found so far across these Western European countries, we deem it appropriate to conduct further in-depth analysis of the factors to look for potential differences, which might be rather significant for the overall analysis.

We shall conduct this analysis according to the following criteria:

- active vs. reactive internationalization;
- internationalization strategy;
- percentage of sales originating from activity abroad;
- business ownership (family vs. non-family); and
- subcontracting operations.

Success factors and internationalization approach

Analysing the active vs. reactive behaviour of internationalization across countries we find the respondents clustered in the active and the reactive groups – rather than according to their nationalities (Figure 3.5). The SMEs actively engaged abroad stress the importance of quality management, their sales staff and their ability to solve technical problems. This result is in line with conventional wisdom, which assumes that the activity and dynamics developed abroad originate from the people (especially in management and marketing staff) involved and their respective abilities.

The Swiss companies are more reactively engaged abroad, and think of factors such as reliability of delivery, customer relations and customer service to be of more importance in determining success.

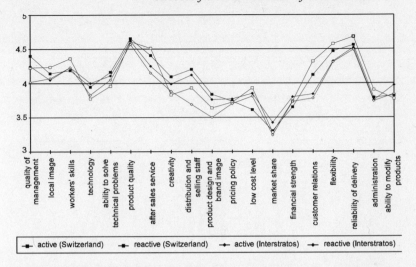

1 = no importance; 2 = low importance; 3 = medium importance; 4 = high importance; 5 = very high importance
(Interstratos-countries without Switzerland 1993: N = 1677; Switzerland 1993: N = 400)

Figure 3.5 Success factors according to internationalization approach

Success factors and internationalization strategy

Here it seems rather obvious that factors for success would be rated highly, depending upon whether the SME is engaged in the importing business or is exporting.

SMEs in the importing business rate flexibility, reliability of delivery, and product quality (Figure 3.6) to be significant success factors; factors which one would expect to find with acquiring and buying businesses.

Remarkably, we do find the same factors to be thought of as success factors (Figure 3.6) with the SMEs engaged in exporting.

Thus, the flow of foreign activity (buy/import vs. sell/export) does not seem to have any influence on the ranking of success factors.

Success factors and percentage of sales from foreign activity

Naturally of increased interest are those SMEs, which have longer records and experience of doing business abroad. This foreign experience is usually reflected in a high percentage of sales originating abroad (more than 60 per cent of total sales). Here we find product quality to be the highest rated success factor (Figure 3.7), in addition to which the Swiss rate customer service highly (after sales) and management quality, two factors which are rated significantly lower

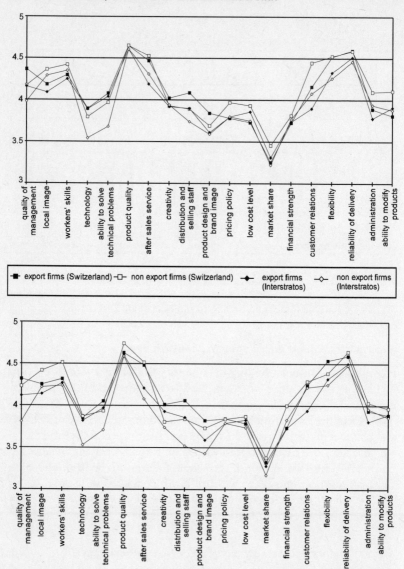

Figure 3.6 Success factors according to internationalization strategy

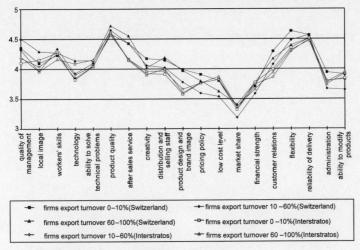

1 = no importance; 2 = low importance; 3 = medium importance; 4 = high importance;
5 = very high importance
(Interstratos-countries without Switzerland 1993: N = 1677; Switzerland 1993: N = 400)

Figure 3.7 Success factors and percentages sales from foreign activity

by the other Western Europeans. Maybe, they perceive the importance of these factors as an already foregone conclusion.

Success factors and business ownership (family vs. non-family)

Surprisingly, we find – in Figure 3.8 – the Swiss Family Businesses to rate the majority of factors significantly more important to their success than do their counterparts in Western Europe. On the top of their list of significant factors we find product quality, customer service (after sales), reliability of delivery and flexibility; the importance of these factors we – by now – know. It is remarkable that the other Western Europeans do tend to rate these factors significantly lower (with the exception of product quality) than the Swiss do.

Success factors and subcontracting operations

Of the four main factors in Figure 3.9 we find product quality and reliability to be of equal importance as success factors. The Swiss also find flexibility and customer service (after sales) to be of weight, whereas their Western European counterparts do express significantly less concern with these two factors.

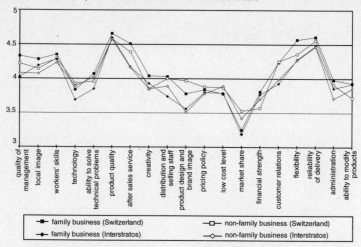

Figure 3.8 Success factors and business ownership (family vs. non-family)

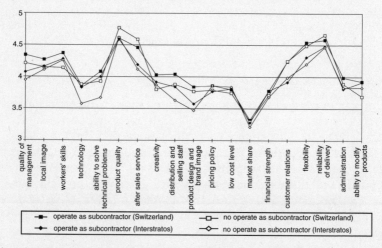

Figure 3.9 Success factors and subcontracting operations

Again, we cannot find a truly sensible interpretation, unless of course, one wants to engage in premature praise and glorification of Swiss entrepreneurs.

Conclusions from the success factor comparisons

The earlier analysis and interpretation (with regard to the importance of success factor, as rated by SME managers), which showed no country specific deviations, was basically confirmed, in spite of our analysis of single factors. Interestingly, we find that the earlier list of seven (out of nineteen) very important success factors, as determined by our aggregated analysis, was increased by only three further factors in our analysis of single factors. These three factors – quality of sales staff, ability to solve technical problems and customer relations – were all found to be significant, dependent upon whether a more active or reactive internationalization strategy was employed.

Thus, we may conclude that of the nineteen tested success factors, approximately half were thought to be of significance, as determined and rated by the SMEs' managers (accounting for over 3,000 firms across Western Europe). The important factors were:

- product quality;
- reliability of delivery;
- flexibility;
- management quality;
- workers' skills;
- customer service (after sales);
- local image;
- quality of sales staff;
- ability to solve technical problems; and
- customer relations.

To pursue our special interest of comparing Swiss SMEs with their Western European counterparts, we do find that our analysis of single factors has made the differences more transparent.

The divergence is not the *difference* of factors, but rather the *degree* of importance which the Swiss attributed to these factors. This observation was made with the factors of percentage of sales from foreign activity, business ownership, and subcontracting operations; whilst the interpretation of these differences remains uncertain. No other significant differences could be found in the cross-country comparisons.

Recapitulating we see that this study was initiated with the clear intention of researching the internationalization process of SMEs. Remarkably we now find that most factors for success, determined within the context of this study, seem to have general relevance and importance for SMEs, as the literature indicates (Pleitner 1988: 14ff;

Küpper 1994: 121ff; Daschmann 1994: 89f). This implies that the factors for success in doing business abroad are the same as the factors for success in general business activity of SMEs. Differences seem only to exist in the weighting of the factors.

SUMMARY

Whilst in this study we were particularly interested in the internationalization process of Swiss SMEs, this study also served the purpose of comparing the current state of the internationalization process of the Swiss SMEs with that of their Western European counterparts.

To put it briefly and somewhat simplified, we do find that the Swiss SMEs – contrary to the macroimage of Switzerland as an export nation – are generally very cautious and hold back in conducting business abroad. This then explains why their Western European counterparts have advanced further in this internationalization process. However, once Swiss SMEs have decided to take the road towards internationalization, they do so whole-heartedly with all necessary respect for the perceived success factors. This approach then causes fewer Swiss SMEs to break off their foreign engagement. Potentially, we believe that the Swiss SMEs may have a healthy respect for the necessary success factors, causing them to hold back and be rather cautious about internationalization in the beginning.

However, we do not want to put too much weight on the differences above, for the Swiss SMEs are fundamentally not behaving much different in the internationalization process, nor do they judge and rate the success factors very differently.

Nevertheless, we may also conclude from these empirical results that the SMEs – in all countries participating in this study – have advanced quite remarkably in the process of internationalization. As a matter of fact, we find the degree of advancement of the internationalization process so highly evolved that we recommend a revision of the classical perception of SMEs, which up to now suggested SMEs were operating merely at the local or regional level.

NOTES

1 A comparison by region shows clearly that Swiss companies – over the past few years – have started to carry out more business outside Europe, particularly in North America and Asia, except for Japan (see Schweiz. Bankverein 1994:1).

2 The paper relies on data from the Interstratos Project (findings for Switzerland and the Interstratos countries as a whole). The chi-square test is used

to determine whether certain attitudes of the Interstratos-population are independent of each other or not. Chi-square was calculated for certain significance levels ($p = 0.1$, $p = 0.05$, $p = 0.01$). The chi-square test for changes in market position (Figure 3.3) and activities in foreign countries (Figure 3.2) showed a multitude of significant differences. For the analysis of the success factors (Figures 3.4, 3.5, 3.7, 3.8, 3.9), with the exception of the differentiated analysis of the success factors according to internationalization strategy (Figure 3.6), we find for the majority of the variables similar significances.

3 See Figure 3.2.
4 Pleitner 1995: 535–537.
5 This circumstance is not only typical of the Swiss: The choice of a combination of various strategies (e.g. export, cooperation with foreign partners, and capital investments abroad) was also found in an American study, conducted in the State of Indiana (Baird *et al.* 1994: 48).
6 See Hall, 1987. This is particularly emphasized in the PIMS studies (e.g. Buzzell and Gale 1987: 9), but also in studies of the Boston Consulting Group (e.g. Henderson 1972: 19ff).

REFERENCES

Baird, I.S., Lyles, M.A. and Orris, J.B. (1994) 'The Choice of International Strategies by Small Businesses', *Journal of Small Business Management*, January.

Bamberger, I. and Pleitner, H.J. (eds) (1988) *Strategische Ausrichtung kleiner und mittlerer Unternehmen*, Sonderheft 3 Internationales Gewerbearchiv, Berlin/ München/ St. Gallen.

Borner, S. *et al.* (1991) *Internationale Wettbewerbsvorteile: Ein Strategisches Konzept für die Schweiz*, Frankfurt am Main.

Brunner, J. and Habersaat, M. (1994) 'Auslandsorientierung und Unternehmungspolitik schweizerischer Klein-und Mittelunternehmungen', in Pleitner, H.J: (ed.) *Ergebnisse der Erhebung 1991–1993 in fünf Branche*. Schweizerisches Institut für gewerbliche Wirtschaft, St. Gallen.

Bundesminister für wirtschaftliche Angelegenheiten: Bericht über die Situation der kleinen und mittleren Unternehmungen der gewerblichen Wirtschaft, Wien 1989 and 1991.

Buzzell, R.D. and Gale, B.T. (1987) *The PIMS–Principles – Linking Strategy to Performance*, New York: Free Press.

Daschmann, H.-A. (1994) *Erfolgsfaktoren mittelständischer Unternehmen*, Stuttgart: Schäffer-Poeschel.

Gaugler, E. and Gantner, R. (1995/2) 'Der schwierige Schritt über die Grenze. Internationale Aktivitäten mittelständischer Unternehmen', *Blick durch die Wirtschaft*, FAZ, p. 7.

Hall, G. (1987) 'When does Market Share matter?', *Journal of Economic Studies*, 16, 4.

Henderson, B.D. (1972) *Perspectives on Experience*, Boston: Beacon Press.

Hurni, B. (1995/2) 'Beobachtungsnetz für Klein- und Mittelunternehmen', *Internationales Gewerbearchiv*, p. 129.

Johanson, J. and Wiederheim, P.F. (1975) 'The Internationalization of the Firm', *Journal of Management Studies*, pp. 305–22.

62   H.J. Pleitner, J. Brunner and M. Habersaat

Küpper, H.-U. (1994) 'Erfolgsfaktoren mittelständischer Unternehmen', in H.J. Pleitner (ed.) *Structures and Strategies in Small and Medium-sized Enterprises as Impacts of Economic Recovery*. Papers presented to the 'Rencontres de St. Gall', pp. 115–24.

Meissner, H.G. and Gerber, S. (1980/3) 'Die Auslandsinvestition als Entscheidungsproblem', *Betriebswirtschaftliche Forschung und Praxis (BFuP)*, pp. 217–28.

Mugler, J. and Miesenböck, K.J. (1990/1) 'Bestimmungsfaktoren der Exportintensität von Gewerbebetrieben', *Internationales Gewerbearchiv*, pp. 1–17.

Pleitner, H.J. (1985) 'Auslandsbetätigung Kleiner Betriebe – Optionen und Restriktionen', in H.J. Pleitner and W. Sertl (eds) *Führung kleiner und Mittlerer Unternehmen*, München: Institut für Handwekswirtschaft, pp. 145–62.

Pleitner, H.J. (1988) 'Künftige Erfolgsfaktoren für das Gewerbe', in J. Mugler (ed.) *Internationales Gewerbeforum*, Band III, Wien, pp. 13–25.

Pleitner, H.J. (1995) 'Internationalisierung schweizerischer Klein- und Mittelunternehmen: Wettbewerbsbedingungen und Unternehmenspolitik im Internationalisierungsprozess', in H. Stiegler (ed.) *Erfolgsotentiale für Klein- und Mittelunternehmen*, Linz: Trauner Universitätsverlag, pp. 525–54.

Pleitner, H.J. (ed.) (1994) 'Auslandsorientierung und Unternehmungspolitik schweizerischer Klein- und Mittelunternehmen', in *Ergebnisse der Erhebung 1991–1993 in fünf Branchen*, Schweizerisches Institut für gewerbliche Wirtschaft, St. Gallen.

Pleitner, H.J. and Müller, B. (1990/4) 'Die Internationalisierung schweizerischer Klein- und Mittelunternehmen im Hinblick auf die Europäische Integration', *Internationales Gewerbearchiv*, pp. 221–35.

Schweizerischer Bankverein (1994) 'Neue Chancen für die Exportwirtschaft', *Der Schlüssel zur Schweizer Wirtschaft*, III/ July, p. 1.

Steinmann, H., Kumar, B. and Wasner, A. (1981) 'Der Internationalisierungsprozess von Mittelunternehmen', in E. Pausenberger (ed.) *Internationales Management. Ansätze und Ergebnisse betriebswirtschaftlicher Forschung*, Stuttgart: Schäffer Poeschel, pp. 107–27.

Wüthrich, H.A. and Winter, W.B. (1994/95) 'Die Wettbewerbskraft globaler Unternehmen', *Die Unternehmung*, pp. 303–22.

4 Entrepreneurial profiles and strategies for the larger market[1]

Erwin A. Fröhlich and J. Hanns Pichler

INTRODUCTION

Entrepreneurial attitudes such as 'willingness to change' and 'taking risks' may be considered crucial prerequisites for success, especially under conditions of dynamic change as, for example, enlargement of markets in the process of EU integration with resulting challenges for necessary adjustments and strategic responses. The question, thus, arises, which, in such an environment, might be the more adaptive or appropriate entrepreneurial 'type'.

Recent research on entrepreneurship seems to ascertain that, in essence, a mix of more specific profiles or 'types' of entrepreneurs prevails; a mix – if going by the original Stratos typology (cf. Fröhlich and Pichler 1988) and followed up by the Interstratos study – referring to pioneers (with distinct openness to change and risk), to organizers (with more pronounced administrative-executive strengths), to allrounders (as a kind of 'jacks-of-all-trades', without really outstanding strengths) and finally to routineers (as representing the more risk averse 'rentier').

Specifics as to methodological aspects and background of both the Stratos and Interstratos research projects are summarized in the following overview.

Stratos	Interstratos
• Acronyms standing for:	
*Stra*tegic *O*rientation of *S*mall European Businesses	*Inter*nationalization of *Stra*tegic Orientations of European *S*mall and Medium Enterprises
• Participating countries:	
Austria	Austria
Belgium	Belgium
Finland	Finland
France	Norway

Germany
UK
Switzerland
The Netherlands

Sweden
UK*
Switzerland
The Netherlands

● Selected industries or sectors:

Textiles/clothing
Electronics
Food

Textiles/clothing
Electronics
Food
Metal/machinery
Furniture making

● Stratification of sampling:

Stratified random sample pertaining to 5 size classes, by number of employees (full time equivalents): 1–9, 10–19, 20–49, 50–99, 100–499

● Sampling and sample size:

Individual in depth interviews
(approx. 1230 entrepreneurs)

Mailed questionnaire
(approx. 3000 responses)

● Data base (questionnaire):

Approx. 600 variables
(thereof on values and attitudes 85)
referring to period 1983–1985

Approx. 200 variables
(thereof on values and attitudes 12,
condensed into 'profiles')
referring to samples 91/92/93/94/95

● Methodological approach:

Cross section analyses

Longitudinal approach (panels and
repeated cross section analyses)

Measuring significance by chi-square tests, and distribution by standard deviation

● Cluster derived entrepreneurial 'types':

2 basic: 'pioneer', 'organizer'
2 derived (mixed): 'allrounder',
'routineer'

2 basic: 'pioneer' and 'organizer'

Fastclus-procedure/SAS program package

EDP – common data base, Institute of Small Business Research (IfG), Vienna

Note*: Questions designed to identify types of entrepreneurs by their values and attitudes were omitted from the UK study.

ATTITUDES AND STRATEGIC RESPONSES BY ENTREPRENEURIAL 'TYPES'

Both the Stratos and Interstratos projects attempt to position the small business entrepreneur as seen in his or her comprehensive role as the very centre of activities.

In depicting the 'proper entrepreneurial type for the larger market', recent Interstratos results seem to point towards the pioneers with certain limitations, however, as regards phase management, whereby specific strengths have to be judged in the context of different phases of business life-cycles (no 'men for all seasons').

Based on that, the following questions emerged as being pertinent in the context of this investigation:

- what do entrepreneurial 'profiles' look like, and are there any distinct patterns of change?;
- how do personal characteristics and social or family ties influence patterns of entrepreneurial 'profiles'?;
- in what ways do the values and attitudes of 'pioneers' and 'organizers' differ?;
- which entrepreneurial 'type' is more inclined to cooperate?; and
- how do 'organizers' and 'pioneers' react to market changes in the context of business life-cycles?

WHAT DO ENTREPRENEURIAL 'PROFILES' LOOK LIKE, AND ARE THERE ANY DISTINCT PATTERNS OF CHANGE?

Empirical findings reveal considerable differences (three out of twelve indicators) with regard to entrepreneurial values and attitudes as shown in Figure 4.1.

		1	2	3	4	5
1	Government should not restrict competition, even not interfere through incentives			•	⊗	
2	Professional bodies and similar organizations should provide assistance to their members only			•	⊗	
3	Changes in a business should be avoided at all costs	•	⊗			
4	A firm should not leave the location where it is established			• ⊗		
5	Jobs should be clearly described and defined in detail			•	⊗	
6	Managers should plan rather than follow their intuition			•	⊗	
7	Firms should only introduce proven office procedures and production techniques			•	⊗	
8	In family-owned businesses management should stay in family hands			•⊗		
9	Small firms should not hesitate to do business with large firms				•⊗	
10	Small business managers should take personal responsibility for the recruitment of all employees				•⊗	
11	A manager should consider ethical principles in his behaviour			·	•⊗	
12	Business should take precedence over family life			•⊗		

Legend:	Ranking:	3 – no opinion
• = pioneer	1 – strongly disagree	4 – agree
⊗ = organizer	2 – disagree	5 – strongly agree

Figure 4.1 Profile of entrepreneurial values and attitudes of pioneers and organizers

Source: IfG-graph[1] Interstratos, total sample[2]

Table 4.1 Changes in patterns of types of entrepreneurs by countries, sectors and size classes, 1991–1995

	Pioneers					Organizers Percentage of sample					Total sample N				
	1991	1992	1993	1994	1995	1991	1992	1993	1994	1995	1991	1992	1993	1994	1995
Countries															
Austria	42	44	44	43	40	58	56	56	57	60	472	493	466	442	371
Belgium	26	27	23	31	34	74	73	77	69	66	454	223	273	242	264
Netherlands	49	46	46	–	53	51	54	54	–	47	540	547	500	–	349
Switzerland	63	65	60	63	69	37	35	40	37	31	370	419	364	364	434
Norway	59	56	59	55	58	41	44	41	45	42	323	337	270	299	310
Sweden	70	68	73	70	70	30	32	27	31	30	527	528	517	568	499
Finland	65	65	64	66	63	35	35	36	34	37	297	354	267	258	205
Sectors															
textiles/clothing	51	54	53	55	56	49	46	47	45	44	567	527	492	422	463
electronics	58	64	65	65	63	42	36	35	34	37	553	514	462	365	397
food	50	51	50	54	52	50	49	50	46	48	561	621	515	407	464
furniture making	50	50	48	52	55	50	50	52	48	45	576	535	514	407	472
metal/machinery	53	54	52	57	58	47	46	48	44	42	726	704	674	572	636
Size classes															
1–9 employees	43	45	43	50	48	57	55	57	50	52	622	608	565	446	498
10–19 employees	52	52	46	50	52	48	48	54	50	48	596	594	540	415	461
20–49 employees	51	56	54	54	56	49	44	46	46	44	719	705	667	577	636
50–99 employees	57	59	63	59	61	43	41	37	41	39	548	511	441	383	436
100–499 employees	63	62	66	71	69	37	38	34	30	31	498	483	444	352	401
Mean	53	54	53	56	57	47	46	47	44	43	2,983	2,900	2,631	2,173	2,432

Source: Interstratos update 1996

The profiles of Figure 4.1 result from cluster analyses as repeatedly tested and applied in both Stratos and Interstratos studies; originally comprising 85 value statements in the Stratos questionnaire and subsequently condensed (on the basis of factor analysis) to 12 profile indicators for the purposes of Interstratos (see also p. 64).

Differing entrepreneurial values and attitudes – as 'typified' by pioneers and organizers – reveal the pattern of Table 4.1.

Disaggregation by firm size suggests that – not quite unexpectedly – fewer pioneers are found in the smaller size classes, where apparently more of the strengths of the allrounders are required.

When differentiated by countries, more pioneers can be found both in the rather dynamic sectors (such as electronics) and in the relatively wealthy countries (Sweden, Switzerland); changes concerning entrepreneurial profiles also become obvious over the four year observation period, but are not to be explained solely by structural influences.

HOW PERSONAL CHARACTERISTICS AND SOCIAL OR FAMILY TIES TEND TO INFLUENCE PATTERNS OF ENTREPRENEURIAL 'PROFILES'

The underlying distinctive factors which will be considered are gender, age and family capital.

As to gender, the widely held view that male entrepreneurs correlate more strongly with the dynamic pioneers, and female entrepreneurs with the more stability oriented organizers no longer seems to be supported by empirical findings. This may partly be due to the relatively small share of female entrepreneurs, averaging only around 10 per cent in the sample (thus, representing a kind of 'elite'). However, even in sectors with female shares of up to 15 per cent (as in textiles or quite generally across sectors in Austria and Finland), females figure more or less equally among pioneers and organizers.

The age of entrepreneurs – somewhat unexpectedly – turns out as being not really significant. Between the younger age cohort and the pioneers on the one hand, and the older more 'seasoned' segment and the organizers (assumed as tending toward greater caution in business conduct) on the other only weak correlations are to be discerned.

As to the role of family capital, related empirical data corroborate earlier Stratos findings that entrepreneurs with higher shares of equity or family funds at stake tend to be rather averse to changes or risks as demonstrated in Table 4.2.

Table 4.2 Share of family businesses* according to types of entrepreneurs by countries, sectors and size classes, 1991–1995

	Pioneers					Organizers Percentage of sample					Total sample N				
	1991	1992	1993	1994	1995	1991	1992	1993	1994	1995	1991	1992	1993	1994	1995
Countries															
Austria	79	77	75	73	72	82	84	83	83	87	461	483	454	424	361
Belgium	76	78	73	73	–	79	78	81	87	–	453	222	273	240	–
Netherlands	56	59	54	–	68	65	65	61	–	66	537	535	496	–	349
Switzerland	76	76	78	74	75	72	79	77	70	73	361	413	356	357	425
Norway	52	50	47	48	49	57	52	64	58	56	314	327	260	293	304
Sweden	62	63	60	62	60	73	74	72	71	77	519	514	479	554	491
Finland	57	63	57	61	60	77	72	67	75	67	292	352	263	238	187
Sectors															
textiles/clothing	77	79	69	70	73	81	81	79	86	82	562	528	480	405	394
electronics	54	51	52	52	51	59	55	55	60	59	547	502	449	356	367
food	56	61	58	59	61	73	71	73	70	70	549	602	495	394	391
furniture making	76	77	76	80	74	80	81	80	83	80	565	522	505	400	421
metal/machinery	60	63	62	62	63	71	70	71	73	70	714	692	652	551	544
Size classes															
1–9 employees	79	79	83	79	79	83	82	78	85	83	612	600	548	436	434
10–19 employees	73	76	76	72	72	78	77	77	82	79	584	587	527	402	422
20–49 employees	68	68	64	68	71	74	73	77	77	73	707	685	646	554	539
50–99 employees	57	55	57	62	59	70	72	69	62	60	542	502	427	371	380
100–499 employees	45	51	40	43	42	48	48	50	56	54	492	472	433	343	342
Mean	64	66	63	64	65	73	72	73	75	73	2,937	2,846	2,581	2,106	2,117

Note:* Family equity > 50 per cent of total equity
Source: Interstratos update 1996

DIFFERENCES BETWEEN THE VALUES AND ATTITUDES OF PIONEERS AND ORGANIZERS

In addressing this particular question, about half of the indicators turn out to be more type-specific:

- three distinctly differing type-specific values and attitudes (as relating to Figure 4.1 above) seem to depict particular strengths of organizers (with regard especially to personnel management, planning and technology); and
- two further indicators seem to refer more specifically to typical features of pioneers (such as a more prevalent sense and drive for change, entailing also higher risks).

Among the less type-specific indicators, attitudes towards 'ethical principles' might be indicative of rather 'neutral' behavioural patterns, irrespective of demonstrating more dynamic-intuitive (pioneering) or more administrative-static (organizing) entrepreneurial strengths.

In turning to personnel or human resource management (formalized, e.g. by way of job descriptions), it would appear that too rigid or clear-cut descriptions, are seen to be counterproductive by impeding flexibility and adaptive capacities. See Table 4.3.

Similarly on attitudes towards planning versus intuition, the latter quite generally is not being considered a weakness in managing small businesses; positive entrepreneurial attitudes towards planning should not be overestimated. See Table 4.4.

A further seemingly type-specific indicator relates to attitudes towards innovation versus tradition. Here, the close interrelationship between business life-cycles on the one hand and types of entrepreneurs on the other becomes rather obvious (see also the section beginning on p. 77). Tables 4.5 and 4.6 illustrate attitudes towards other aspects of conservatism and radicalism.

Indicators on willingness to change and innovative drive show relatively minor deviations. They relate directly, however, to the very basic types (the pioneers and the organizers) referred to throughout the sub-samples and, thus, even smaller differences are worthy of note, since the respective indicators aim right at the centre of entrepreneurial attitudes (such as being more dynamic or more stability minded; being more progressive or more conservative).

Similar differences are to be discerned with respect to attitudes towards internationalization strategies (see Table 4.7); they also apply to the various sub-samples, disregarding specific phases connected with business life-cycles or changing market conditions.

Table 4.3 Attitudes towards the statement 'Jobs should be clearly described and defined in detail'

| | Pioneers | | | | | Organizers | | | | |
| | Means: 1 = strongly disagree ... 5 = fully agree | | | | | | | | | |
	1991	1992	1993	1994	1995	1991	1992	1993	1994	1995
Countries										
Austria	2.3	2.3	2.4	2.2	2.2	3.4	3.4	3.4	3.4	3.4
Belgium	2.1	2.1	2.3	2.1	2.2	3.5	3.5	3.7	3.4	3.4
Netherlands	2.3	2.4	2.2	–	2.2	3.6	3.6	3.4	–	3.6
Switzerland	2.3	2.3	2.4	2.3	2.3	3.6	3.4	3.4	3.5	3.5
Norway	2.8	2.9	2.8	2.9	2.7	3.9	3.9	3.9	3.9	3.8
Sweden	2.8	2.6	2.7	2.8	2.7	4.0	4.1	4.0	3.9	3.9
Finland	2.4	2.1	2.0	2.1	1.9	3.5	3.6	3.6	3.3	3.5
Sectors										
textiles/clothing	2.5	2.4	2.5	2.6	2.4	3.6	3.6	3.6	3.5	3.4
electronics	2.6	2.5	2.5	2.4	2.3	3.5	3.7	3.5	3.6	3.6
food	2.5	2.5	2.4	2.6	2.5	3.8	3.6	3.6	3.6	3.6
furniture making	2.4	2.4	2.4	2.5	2.4	3.6	3.7	3.6	3.5	3.6
metal/machinery	2.5	2.3	2.4	2.5	2.3	3.6	3.6	3.5	3.5	3.6
Size classes										
1–9 employees	2.4	2.4	2.5	2.6	2.4	3.5	3.5	3.4	3.4	3.5
10–19 employees	2.6	2.5	2.5	2.7	2.4	3.6	3.6	3.6	3.5	3.6
20–49 employees	2.6	2.4	2.5	2.5	2.5	3.7	3.6	3.6	3.7	3.6
50–99 employees	2.5	2.4	2.4	2.5	2.3	3.7	3.7	3.7	3.6	3.6
100–499 employees	2.4	2.3	2.4	2.2	2.3	3.7	3.8	3.7	3.7	3.6
Mean	2.5	2.4	2.4	2.5	2.4	3.6	3.6	3.6	3.6	3.6

Source: Interstratos update 1996

Table 4.4 Attitude towards the statement 'Managers should plan rather than follow their intuition'

| | Pioneers | | | | | Organizers | | | | |
| | Means: 1 = strongly disagree ... 5 = fully agree | | | | | | | | | |
	1991	1992	1993	1994	1995	1991	1992	1993	1994	1995
Countries										
Austria	3.1	3.1	2.8	3.0	3.1	4.0	3.9	3.6	3.9	3.9
Belgium	3.1	3.0	3.0	3.2	2.8	3.9	3.9	3.9	3.9	3.9
Netherlands	2.6	2.5	2.5	–	2.5	3.7	3.7	3.6	–	3.6
Switzerland	2.8	2.8	2.8	2.9	2.8	3.8	3.5	3.8	3.8	3.7
Norway	3.2	3.2	3.2	3.1	3.1	4.1	3.9	3.9	4.0	4.0
Sweden	2.2	2.2	2.3	2.2	2.3	3.4	3.2	3.2	3.1	3.1
Finland	2.6	2.6	2.6	2.6	2.6	3.8	3.7	3.6	3.6	3.6
Sectors										
textiles/clothing	2.6	2.6	2.6	2.7	2.8	3.8	3.6	3.5	3.6	3.6
electronics	2.7	2.7	2.7	2.7	2.6	3.7	3.7	3.7	3.7	3.7
food	2.7	2.7	2.7	2.9	2.6	3.9	3.7	3.7	3.8	3.7
furniture making	2.7	2.6	2.6	2.7	2.7	3.8	3.7	3.7	3.8	3.8
metal/machinery	2.8	2.8	2.7	2.6	2.7	3.9	3.7	3.7	3.7	3.8
Size classes:										
1–9 employees	2.5	2.5	2.5	2.5	2.5	3.7	3.7	3.5	3.6	3.6
10–19 employees	2.6	2.6	2.6	2.8	2.6	3.9	3.6	3.5	3.7	3.7
20–49 employees	2.6	2.7	2.6	2.7	2.7	3.9	3.7	3.8	3.8	3.7
50–99 employees	2.9	2.8	2.7	2.8	2.6	3.9	3.7	3.9	3.8	3.8
100–499 employees	2.9	2.7	2.8	2.8	2.9	4.0	3.9	3.9	3.8	3.8
Mean	2.7	2.7	2.6	2.7	2.7	3.8	3.7	3.7	3.7	3.7

Source: Interstratos update 1996

Table 4.5 Attitudes towards the statement 'Firms should only introduce proven office procedures and production techniques'

	Pioneers					Organizers				
	Means: 1 = strongly disagree ... 5 = fully agree									
	1991	*1992*	*1993*	*1994*	*1995*	*1991*	*1992*	*1993*	*1994*	*1995*
Countries										
Austria	2.1	2.2	2.3	2.2	2.3	3.3	3.2	3.5	3.3	3.4
Belgium	2.9	3.1	2.7	2.7	2.6	3.9	4.0	3.8	3.9	3.7
Netherlands	3.3	3.4	3.3	–	3.5	4.2	4.2	4.1	–	4.1
Switzerland	2.2	2.3	2.2	2.2	2.2	3.4	3.3	3.3	3.4	3.5
Norway	2.2	2.2	2.3	2.3	2.3	3.3	3.3	3.5	3.4	3.3
Sweden	1.9	1.9	1.8	1.8	1.9	3.0	3.2	3.1	2.9	3.0
Finland	2.4	2.4	2.5	2.3	2.4	3.7	3.6	3.5	3.5	3.5
Sectors										
textiles/clothing	2.3	2.3	2.4	2.1	2.3	3.6	3.6	3.7	3.4	3.5
electronics	2.4	2.4	2.4	2.1	2.3	3.6	3.7	3.7	3.4	3.6
food	2.4	2.4	2.4	2.2	2.3	3.6	3.5	3.6	3.4	3.5
furniture making	2.4	2.4	2.3	2.1	2.4	3.6	3.6	3.6	3.4	3.5
metal/machinery	2.4	2.4	2.4	2.2	2.4	3.7	3.6	3.6	3.4	3.5
Size classes										
1–9 employees	2.3	2.4	2.4	2.1	2.4	3.6	3.5	3.5	3.3	3.5
10–19 employees	2.4	2.4	2.3	2.2	2.4	3.6	3.6	3.6	3.3	3.5
20–49 employees	2.5	2.5	2.4	2.1	2.3	3.6	3.6	3.7	3.4	3.5
50–99 employees	2.4	2.4	2.4	2.2	2.4	3.8	3.6	3.6	3.6	3.5
100–499 employees	2.3	2.2	2.4	2.1	2.3	3.7	3.6	3.8	3.4	3.5
Mean	2.4	2.4	2.4	2.1	2.4	3.6	3.6	3.6	3.4	3.5

Source: Interstratos update 1996

Table 4.6 Attitudes towards the statement 'Changes in a business should be avoided at all costs'

	Pioneers					Organizers				
	Means: 1 = strongly disagree ... 5 = fully agree									
	1991	*1992*	*1993*	*1994*	*1995*	*1991*	*1992*	*1993*	*1994*	*1995*
Countries										
Austria	1.4	1.6	1.7	1.5	1.4	2.4	2.3	2.6	2.3	2.2
Belgium	1.8	1.8	1.5	1.5	1.6	2.3	2.3	2.1	1.9	2.0
Netherlands	1.4	1.4	1.4	–	1.4	1.6	1.8	1.7	–	1.6
Switzerland	1.4	1.4	1.3	1.3	1.3	2.1	2.0	1.9	1.8	2.1
Norway	1.4	1.4	1.3	1.2	1.3	1.7	1.7	1.8	1.7	1.8
Sweden	1.2	1.2	1.1	1.2	1.2	1.8	1.7	1.9	1.8	1.8
Finland	1.4	1.5	1.4	1.6	1.5	2.1	2.0	2.3	2.0	2.0
Sectors										
textiles/clothing	1.5	1.4	1.4	1.3	1.4	2.1	2.0	2.0	1.9	2.0
electronics	1.3	1.3	1.3	1.3	1.3	1.9	1.9	1.9	1.8	1.8
food	1.4	1.4	1.4	1.3	1.3	2.1	2.0	2.2	2.0	1.9
furniture making	1.4	1.4	1.4	1.3	1.3	2.1	2.0	2.1	2.0	1.9
metal/machinery	1.4	1.4	1.4	1.4	1.4	2.0	1.9	2.0	2.0	1.9
Size classes										
1–9 employees	1.5	1.5	1.4	1.5	1.5	2.3	2.2	2.3	2.2	2.1
10–19 employees	1.5	1.4	1.5	1.4	1.4	2.1	2.0	2.2	2.0	2.0
20–49 employees	1.3	1.4	1.3	1.3	1.3	2.0	1.9	2.0	1.9	2.0
50–99 employees	1.4	1.4	1.4	1.2	1.3	1.8	1.9	1.8	1.8	1.7
100–499 employees	1.3	1.3	1.2	1.2	1.2	1.8	1.6	1.7	1.6	1.7
Mean	1.4	1.4	1.4	1.3	1.3	2.0	2.0	2.1	2.0	1.9

Source: Interstratos update 1996

Table 4.7 Attitudes towards the statement 'A firm should not leave the region where it is established'

	Pioneers					Organizers				
	Means: 1 = strongly disagree ... 5 = fully agree									
	1991	1992	1993	1994	1995	1991	1992	1993	1994	1995
Countries										
Austria	1.6	1.8	1.7	1.7	1.8	2.7	2.7	2.7	2.6	2.6
Belgium	1.6	1.6	1.8	1.8	1.9	2.0	2.0	2.7	2.6	2.5
Netherlands	1.9	1.8	1.8	–	1.8	2.3	2.3	2.5	–	2.5
Switzerland	2.0	1.9	1.8	1.9	1.9	2.9	2.8	2.6	2.6	2.7
Norway	2.2	2.4	2.2	2.4	2.2	2.8	2.8	2.8	2.8	2.9
Sweden	1.7	1.8	1.7	1.6	1.6	2.8	2.7	2.6	2.7	2.6
Finland	1.6	1.7	1.7	1.9	1.7	2.6	2.5	2.5	2.6	2.5
Sectors										
textiles/clothing	1.9	1.9	1.8	1.9	1.8	2.5	2.6	2.7	2.7	2.6
electronics	1.7	1.8	1.7	1.8	1.9	2.4	2.4	2.4	2.3	2.6
food	1.8	1.8	1.8	1.8	1.8	2.5	2.7	2.7	2.6	2.6
furniture making	1.8	1.9	1.7	1.9	1.8	2.5	2.6	2.6	2.7	2.6
metal/machinery	1.8	1.8	1.8	1.8	1.8	2.5	2.4	2.6	2.7	2.5
Size classes										
1–9 employees	1.8	1.8	1.8	2.0	1.9	2.8	2.8	2.8	2.8	2.7
10–19 employees	1.9	2.0	1.8	2.0	1.9	2.6	2.5	2.7	2.6	2.6
20–49 employees	1.8	1.8	1.7	1.8	1.8	2.4	2.5	2.6	2.6	2.7
50–99 employees	1.8	1.9	1.8	1.8	1.9	2.3	2.4	2.4	2.7	2.5
100–499 employees	1.7	1.7	1.7	1.7	1.7	2.3	2.4	2.4	2.4	2.5
Mean	1.8	1.8	1.8	1.8	1.8	2.5	2.5	2.6	2.6	2.6

Source: Interstratos update 1996

Table 4.8 Attitudes towards the statement 'A manager should consider ethical principles in his behaviour'

	Pioneers					Organizers				
	Means: 1 = strongly disagree ... 5 = fully agree									
	1991	1992	1993	1994	1995	1991	1992	1993	1994	1995
Countries										
Austria	3.9	3.7	3.8	3.7	3.7	3.9	3.9	3.9	3.8	3.9
Belgium	4.0	4.1	4.2	4.3	4.3	4.1	4.1	4.1	4.0	4.1
Netherlands	4.0	3.9	4.1	–	4.0	4.1	4.0	4.0	–	4.0
Switzerland	4.0	3.9	–	4.0	3.9	4.2	4.1	–	4.0	3.9
Norway	4.1	4.1	4.1	4.2	4.2	4.1	3.9	4.0	4.1	4.0
Sweden	3.6	3.7	3.7	3.8	3.8	3.8	3.9	3.7	3.9	4.0
Finland	4.0	3.9	4.0	3.9	3.8	3.9	3.9	3.9	3.8	3.9
Sectors										
textiles/clothing	3.8	3.8	3.9	3.8	3.9	3.9	3.8	3.9	4.0	3.9
electronics	4.0	4.0	4.0	4.0	4.1	4.1	4.1	4.0	3.8	4.1
food	3.8	3.8	3.9	4.0	3.8	4.0	4.0	3.9	4.0	3.9
furniture making	3.9	3.8	3.8	3.7	3.7	4.0	4.0	3.8	3.9	4.0
metal/machinery	3.9	3.9	4.0	3.9	4.0	4.0	4.0	4.0	3.9	4.0
Size classes										
1–9 employees	3.7	3.7	3.8	3.5	3.7	4.0	3.9	3.8	3.8	3.9
10–19 employees	3.7	3.6	3.7	3.8	3.8	4.0	3.9	3.8	3.9	3.9
20–49 employees	3.9	3.9	3.9	3.9	3.9	4.0	4.0	4.0	3.9	4.0
50–99 employees	4.0	3.9	4.0	4.1	4.0	4.1	4.1	4.1	4.0	4.1
100–499 employees	4.0	4.1	4.2	4.1	4.2	4.1	4.2	4.1	4.2	4.1
Mean	3.9	3.9	3.9	3.9	3.9	4.0	4.0	3.9	3.9	4.0

Source: Interstratos update 1996

Table 4.9 Attitudes towards the statement 'A manager should consider ethical principles in his behaviour' (percentage of sample in each of three categories)

	Contra					Undecided					Pro				
	1991	1992	1993	1994	1995	1991	1992	1993	1994	1995	1991	1992	1993	1994	1995
Countries															
Austria	4	6	6	9	6	22	20	24	20	23	74	74	70	71	70
Belgium	2	2	2	3	3	12	12	15	15	10	85	86	83	82	87
Netherlands	3	4	3	–	4	12	16	13	–	14	85	80	84	–	82
Switzerland	4	6	–	6	5	17	15	–	10	16	79	79	–	84	78
Norway	3	3	2	2	2	13	12	14	8	8	85	84	85	90	90
Sweden	15	11	13	11	12	31	30	26	27	24	54	59	61	63	64
Finland	9	10	10	13	9	13	13	9	14	16	78	76	81	73	74
Sectors															
textiles/clothing	6	8	6	8	7	20	22	20	17	19	74	69	74	76	74
electronics	5	5	4	7	4	14	17	17	15	15	82	79	79	78	81
food	6	7	7	8	9	19	16	17	16	16	75	76	75	76	76
furniture making	6	8	8	8	7	19	18	20	23	20	75	74	72	69	73
metal/machinery	6	5	6	8	4	18	17	17	16	16	76	78	77	76	80
Size classes															
1–9 employees	6	6	6	11	7	22	24	26	25	26	72	70	68	64	66
10–19 employees	7	9	9	8	9	21	24	24	21	19	72	68	68	71	72
20–49 employees	6	6	8	8	6	18	16	15	17	17	77	77	77	76	77
50–99 employees	5	6	5	7	5	14	13	13	13	11	81	82	82	79	83
100–499 employees	4	5	3	4	4	14	12	10	8	10	82	83	87	87	86
Type of entrepreneurs															
Pioneers	8	9	9	10	8	18	18	16	16	16	74	73	76	74	76
Organizers	3	4	4	5	4	18	17	21	18	18	79	78	75	76	78
Means	6	7	6	8	6	18	18	18	17	17	76	75	76	75	77

Source: Interstratos update 1996

Table 4.10 Frequency of pioneers and organizers cooperating with *domestic partners at home* in different fields, 1991–1995

	Pioneers					Organizers Percentage					Total N				
	1991	1992	1993	1994	1995	1991	1992	1993	1994	1995	1991	1992	1993	1994	1995
Sales	37	27	45	34	33	28	26	35	35	30	2,106	1,973	1,575	1,617	1,834
Extension of product-range	33	29	41	33	31	25	25	30	29	27	2,205	2,135	1,562	1,353	1,832
Manufacture	33	30	38	33	30	25	24	30	31	26	2,196	2,131	1,568	1,617	1,834
Purchase/supply	27	24	29	24	24	20	24	22	25	22	2,184	2,132	1,540	1,592	1,825
Research and development	25	25	27	25	23	18	20	20	19	18	2,187	2,130	1,547	1,332	1,834
Transport/warehousing	24	21	28	24	20	16	19	20	23	17	2,188	2,129	1,525	1,567	1,822
Electronic data processing	19	17	22	21	16	15	16	15	19	12	2,186	2,134	1,526	1,556	1,824
Joint venture (local firm)	2	1	2	1	1	1	0	1	1	1	2,983	2,901	2,657	2,173	2,432

Source: Interstratos update 1996

Table 4.11 Frequency of pioneers and organizers cooperating with *foreign partners abroad* in different fields, 1991–1995

	Pioneers					Organizers Percentage					Total N				
	1991	1992	1993	1994	1995	1991	1992	1993	1994	1995	1991	1992	1993	1994	1995
Sales	29	26	31	28	27	20	23	21	17	18	1,807	1,738	1,499	1,509	1,736
Extension of product-range	25	22	21	17	19	18	17	15	11	13	1,809	1,734	1,482	1,484	1,730
Research and development	14	14	17	11	13	11	12	10	7	8	1,783	1,723	1,468	1,471	1,728
Manufacture	15	13	15	16	14	11	10	11	11	9	1,794	1,731	1,466	1,487	1,729
Purchase/supply	14	14	14	14	12	10	12	11	8	8	1,789	1,725	1,462	1,485	1,722
Joint venture (firm abroad)	8	6	7	7	7	5	4	4	3	3	2,983	2,893	2,630	2,173	2,432

Source: Interstratos update 1996

Table 4.12 Frequency of pioneers and organizers cooperating with *foreign partners at home* in the fields of extension of product-range by sectors, 1991–1995

Industry	Pioneers					Organizers Percentage					Total N				
	1991	1992	1993	1994	1995	1991	1992	1993	1994	1995	1991	1992	1993	1994	1995
textiles/clothing	18	15	15	11	18	20	19	17	8	18	367	327	283	316	320
electronics	26	24	22	17	26	22	28	26	14	18	385	354	254	262	285
food	21	19	13	14	19	19	15	15	12	7	343	377	270	286	339
furniture making	15	10	14	11	11	10	10	11	9	9	364	319	303	294	332
metal/machinery	23	18	24	18	22	21	15	15	11	13	496	478	413	420	487
Total	21	18	19	14	20	18	16	16	11	13	1,955	1,855	1,523	1,578	1,763

Source: Interstratos update 1996

Table 4.13 Frequency of pioneers and organizers cooperating with *domestic partners abroad* in the field of sales by sectors, 1991–1995

Industry	Pioneers					Organizers Percentage					Total N				
	1991	1992	1993	1994	1995	1991	1992	1993	1994	1995	1991	1992	1993	1994	1995
textiles/clothing	12	8	11	13	10	12	10	9	7	13	339	315	266	302	312
electronics	11	15	17	8	9	9	12	13	15	7	345	320	239	251	278
food	10	10	12	11	11	13	16	9	12	7	289	322	261	254	329
furniture making	13	14	16	13	11	8	11	10	15	9	329	297	283	264	314
metal/machinery	18	15	12	11	14	10	13	15	12	12	466	441	395	397	474
Total	13	13	14	11	11	10	12	11	12	10	1,768	1,695	1,444	1,468	1,707

Source: Interstratos update 1996

Indicators to ethical principles turn out to hardly differ at all with respect to the two basic types of pioneers and organizers. Here, however, the answer category 'undecided' may be worth closer scrutiny in order to get behind the obviously quite similar patterns of 'morals' in business conduct which might turn out to be somewhat devious. Tables 4.8 and 4.9 explore these ethical attitudes.

The relatively high share of 'undecided' in responding to ethical principles might indeed imply greater reliance on conveying appropriate value based principles through education and training generally.

ENTREPRENEURIAL TYPE AND COOPERATION

Business cooperation, instead of outright or 'cut-throat' competition, has been an issue addressed in the context of both Stratos and Interstratos. Cooperation strategies also reflect basic entrepreneurial attitudes which, therefore, it would seem relevant to investigate more closely.

If it is assumed that cooperation, as a rule, involves uncertainty (partners not sticking to agreements or turning out to be inefficient), it may be a plausible hypothesis to assume: pioneers rather than organizers should be more open to cooperation, which is supported by empirical findings; stronger inclination towards cooperation on the part of pioneers as against organizers being evident both with respect to domestic partners at home and with respect to foreign partners abroad as is shown in Tables 4.10, 4.11, 4.12 and 4.13.

Not so immediately evident are differing strategies betwwen pioneers and organizers towards cooperation strategies if more specific forms are considered as, e.g. cooperation with foreign partners at home on 'extension of product range' or with domestic partners abroad on sales.

As these results reveal, organizers – especially in the smaller business segments – tend to be more inclined towards cooperation than pioneers which, in turn, may be a reflection of given (possibly critical) phases in the business life-cycle. (Textiles or electronics seem to be cases in point as shown in Table 4.12.)

Again more typical apparently for the organizers than for pioneers seems to be greater caution towards cooperation with domestic partners abroad as, for example, in electronics, in furniture making or metal/machinery (the pioneers quite obviously representing the more 'daring' types).

In summarizing these findings, distinct attitudes towards 'cooperation by types of entrepreneurs' can be observed relating to different entrepreneurial strengths and weaknesses, raising the question as to 'the right man at the right time' with regard to different phases of business life-cycles, especially in small businesses.

ORGANIZERS' AND PIONEERS' REACTIONS TO MARKET CHANGES WITHIN BUSINESS LIFE-CYCLES

As demonstrated when depicting specific attitudes and areas of strategies above, both types, organizers and pioneers, tend to prudently share the risks from various challenges through cooperation with partners thus making use of their respective strengths as illustrated in Figure 4.2.

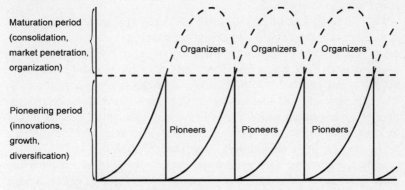

Figure 4.2 Entrepreneurial 'types' and business life-cycle*
Note: * Cf. also Pümpin, C. and Prange, S. (1991); Reckhaus, H.D. (1994)

While it is proving difficult to support implied hypotheses by relevant empirical findings (in depicting, e.g. a more pronounced 'pioneering period' or a more 'mature phase'), certain key indicators – such as growth, growing number of employees, rising turnover or exports, etc. – as related to entrepreneurial 'profiles' might provide a kind of yardstick to facilitate understanding of some of the underlying complexities.

SOME CONCLUSIONS TO BE DRAWN

While in larger enterprises tasks, such as R&D (pioneers) or controlling (organizers), specific job descriptions and profiles are being formulated, smaller enterprises usually have to rely on respective training and/or consulting facilities (as relevant, e.g. for product design, costing and price strategies, for administrative services, production and processing).

In very small (micro) enterprises managerial tasks more or less crystallize in the Marshallian 'Mr. Microcosm' as simply representing the 'centre of activity'; i.e. the entrepreneur acting as his own designer, market analyst, customer consultant, administrator, accountant, controller, industrial engineer etc., and thereby (like the all-rounder) not really excelling in one or two functions but resembling a jack-of-all-trades. Therein also, however, lies a fundamental distinction between the small business entrepreneur and the big business manager or executive.

In identifying entrepreneurial strengths and weaknesses on more personal grounds, value-related attitudinal indicators can serve as instruments for rationalizing underlying inclinations and the related orientations of strategies.

Once having identified characteristic strengths and weaknesses, it would seem more rational to depict a proper adaptive strategy from of a range of possibilities or options, e.g. as regards different forms of cooperation. This holds true not only for the manifold forms of interfirm cooperation (with domestic as well as foreign partners at home or abroad), but also for the appropriate distribution and delegation of management tasks within firms which, in turn, may be linked to prevailing different phases of business life-cycles (be it more the pioneering or the consolidating organization phase).

This, in summary, also underlines that – in the light of a rediscovery of the particular role of the entrepreneur – new fields of research have emerged and need to be investigated further (such as more explicitly bringing out value-based linkages in determining business strategies and decision making). Empirical findings, as demonstrated here, may facilitate rationally locating given entrepreneurial potentials as a

Determinants of an 'adaptive' strategy mix

	Internal	*External*
Education/training	On the job	Job related schooling/ training, workshops/ business services
Consultancy	Conducting firm-based feasibility-, marketing-studies as well as adressing managerial, accounting or controlling problems, etc.	Hiring specialized advice and services (tax consultants, legal advice, business associations etc.)
Business cooperation	Family members Staff	Domestic partners Foreign partners

particular challenge – not the least in a broadened European context – in quest of a future oriented and more specifically small business conducive policy formulation.

Adaptive entrepreneurial policies may follow a prudent 'strategy mix' to compensate for given weaknesses by resorting, for example, to specific education/training facilities, to specialized consulting services or to specific forms of business cooperation as illustrated in the matrix on page 78.

Findings in this respect show that most, in particular smaller-business entrepreneurs, regularly make use of a variety of outside consulting services. In a generally competitive setting and environment, various (generally more pioneering) forms of cooperation strategies seem to prevail over other alternatives to cope with given weaknesses. These may include: more intensive utilization of training facilities, which was sought after by just about 50 per cent of the firms sampled (and of those again only 30 per cent in the smaller and smallest size classes); and cooperation, which seems to be a preferred form of small business strategy. Table 4.14 summarizes our findings in this area.

Table 4.14 Entrepreneurs going for cooperation strategies*

	Total		up to 9 employees (smallest)		100–499 employees (biggest)	
	Pioneers	Organizers	Pioneers	Organizers	Pioneers	Organizers
At home	55	44	49	49	69	30
Abroad	20	10	7	4	38	13
With domestic partners	55	43	49	48	69	30
With foreign partners	22	12	8	5	39	15

Note: * Multiple answers, therefore adding up to more than 100 per cent
Source: Institut für Gewerbe- und Handwerksforschung (IfG), Vienna 1996

Interfirm division or sharing of functions – no matter whether at home or abroad (with domestic or foreign partners) – reflects, in principle, approaches similar to outsourcing, subcontracting or, for that matter, entering any form of business association; the crucial and performance oriented rationale being always that somebody else might do better or more efficiently what the small firm cannot achieve as well by itself.

Thus, in assuming that cooperation strategies evidently do matter, pioneering strengths indeed may turn out more relevant as compared to organizational/administrative talents while keeping in mind, however, given limits of both types. Small businesses of whichever type or profile might quite easily be overchallenged by too forceful or dynamic a tendency towards internationalization. Caution is always sensible and will not, by itself, prevent a venture that is justified on other grounds.

NOTES

1 Based on empirical findings and related data sets under the Interstratos project with participation of small business researchers from eight European countries (cf. p. 63–4). The Vienna Small Business Research Institute (IfG), in particular P. Voithofer, is to be credited for data processing required and related tabulations; country specific (national) data collection, sampling and analyses were supported by the Austrian Science Foundation.
2 Cf. in this context also, relating to Stratos, Fröhlich, E.A. and Pichler, J.H. (1988); The Stratos Group, Strategic Orientations of Small European Businesses, Aldershot, 1990, esp. on 'Values', pp. 34 ff. More recently further: Fröhlich *et al.* (1994), esp. pp. 44 ff. and 232 f.; Haahti, A.J (ed.) (1995) esp. chs. II and V.

REFERENCES

Fröhlich, E. and Pichler, J.H. (1988) Werte und Typen mittelständischer Unternehmer, Beiträge zur ganzheitlichen Wirtschafts- und Gesellschaftslehre, J.H. Pichler (ed.), vol. 8, Berlin: Dunker & Humboldt.

Fröhlich, E.A., Hawranek, P.M., Lettmayr, C.F. and Pichler, J.H. (1994) Manual for Small Industrial Businesses: Project Design and Appraisal, UNIDO General Studies Series, Vienna.

Haahti, A.J. (ed.) (1995) 'Interstratos. Internationalization of Strategic Orientations of European Small and Medium Enterprises', *EIASM Report*, 95–01, Brussels.

Pümpin, C. and Prange, S. (1991) *Management der Unternehmensentwicklung: phasengerechte Führung und der Umgang mit Krisen*, Frankfurt/New York.

Reckhaus, H.D. (1994) *Ein persönlichkeitsbezogener Ansatz zur erfolgreichen Führung von kleinen und mittleren Unternehmen (KMU).* Internationales Gewerbearchiv, Berlin/Munich/St.Gallen.

The Stratos Group (1990) *Strategic Orientations of Small European Businesses*, Avebury, Aldershot: Gower Publishing.

5 International orientation and external resource dependence of Nordic engineering firms

Petri Ahokangas

INTRODUCTION

The Nordic countries in 1993

Of the five Nordic countries – Finland, Denmark, Iceland, Norway, and Sweden – the three Interstratos countries Finland, Norway, and Sweden form together a rather homogeneous group of countries. This is due to the long historical interconnectedness of the area with active mutual trade and rather similar national cultures. In 1993, about 21.5 per cent of the total imports of the area came from within the area and 19.5 per cent of the total exports of the area were sold within the five Nordic countries (Norden i tal 1994). The most important area for exports as well as imports was the European Union with over 50 per cent share of the total trade of the area. Of course, these figures have changed since Finland and Sweden joined the European Union from the beginning of 1995. Other important trading partners include the EFTA countries and North America.

During the early 1990s inflation in Finland, Norway, and Sweden has been low, varying for example in 1992 from 2.0 per cent (Sweden) to 2.1 per cent (Finland) and 2.2 per cent (Norway). However, the economic recession among SMEs has been severe, especially in Finland and Sweden where the number of unemployed increased rapidly after 1990. The impact of the national and international recession could clearly be seen among the internationalizing SMES of the area. For example, not only did the number of firms with international trade outside the Nordic countries decrease slightly during the early 1990s, but also the number of importing firms decreased (Interstratos 1995).

Internationalization and small firms

The traditional internationalization theory (Buckley and Casson 1976; Rugman 1982) states that the internationally active firm has created some kind of firm-specific advantage in its home markets. Then the objective of the international firm is to retain control over the internal resources that have contributed to the firm's success during the internationalization process. However, within small business research it is assumed that the performance of small firms is to a large extent dependent on external conditions, more specifically on resource availability (Miesenböck 1988; Interstratos 1995), since the small firms do not have internally available resources for internationalization. Therefore the internationalization of small firms is understood to take place through the use of external resources. Especially, the network (Johansson and Mattsson 1988; Nyström 1990) and resource-based (Hurry 1994; Tallman and Fladmoe-Lindquist 1994) perspectives on the process of internationalization address the issue of resource availability. In practice the externally available resources can be reached either through cooperation with other firms or through facilities that sell or otherwise provide valuable information for small firms. Fundamentally, the serious question for the small firm is whether to internationalize alone or in cooperation with other firms.

This kind of view emphasizes the strategic behaviour and adaptation of small firms with regard to the use of externally available resources. Alas, it has been argued (Christensen 1991) that this topic has been neglected within small business research. Traditionally the internationalization of small firms is understood as a gradual sequential process consisting of several stages. As the firm enters into a new stage its international commitment and involvement in international marketing activities increases. An example of the stages of internationalization is given by Czinkota and Johnston (1981). According to them the internationalization process consists of the following stages: (1) the unwilling firm; (2) the uninterested firm; (3) the interested firm; (4) the experimenting firm; (5) the semi-experienced small exporter; and (6) the experienced large exporter. In addition to this, the firm is also bound to choose a certain method or mode of operation through which it enters into new markets. These methods include, for example, indirect exporting, direct exporting, licensing, joint ventures or direct investments. Phatak (1983) presents a different type of categorizing for the stages of the internationalization process based on the modes of international operations: (1) the foreign inquiry; (2) the export manager; (3) the export department and direct sales; (4) sales branches and subsidiaries; (5) assembly abroad; (6) production abroad [(a) contract manufacturing, (b) licensing, and (c) investment in manufacturing]; and (7) integration of foreign affiliates.

However in practice, SMEs do not necessarily operate according to the theoretical stage model of internationalization, but use different operations or activities simultaneously – irrespective of any more or less theoretical model. For the analysis, Luostarinen and Hellman's (1993) definition of holistic internationalization process is adopted. This model is based on the study of Finnish small firms. The advantage of the model is that its basic idea leaves more degrees of freedom for the researcher to study the content of international operations on the firm level than do other models of internationalization processes. Their model includes four stages:

1 Domestic stage (no international operations)
2 Inward stage (technology transfer or import of raw materials and components)
3 Outward stage: (a) Outward processes (exporting, sales subsidiary, subcontracting, contract manufacturing, licensing, manufacturing subsidiary); and (b) Cooperation processes (import of saleable goods, domestic joint venture with foreign partner, import of subcontracted components, contract manufactured goods, licensed products, import from manufacturing subsidiary)
4 Cooperation stage (cooperation agreement on manufacturing, cooperation on purchasing, cooperation on R&D).

In summary, it may be stated that internationalization is a process of both inward and outward type activities. Strategically relevant information for internationalization is acquired not only by acting in the markets and learning from experience but especially by cooperative activities and by using other external information sources available for the firms. From the network perspective the strategy of the firm can be characterized by the need to (1) minimize the need of knowledge development, (2) minimize the need of network adjustment, and (3) utilize the established network positions (Johansson and Mattsson 1988). Since both the firm and the environment can be defined by resources (Conner 1991; Rautkylä 1991) the firm can be said to be dependent on its key internal and key external resources (Gibb and Scott 1985). From the firm perspective the network provides the external resources needed for internationalization through interaction. Thus, strategically important interaction may take place both in domestic and foreign markets or through counterparts in domestic and foreign networks.

Purpose of the analysis

The purpose of this analysis is to explore and discuss the relationship between (1) the firm's international orientation and (2) the firm's dependence on externally available resources. The firm's international orientation is measured by export strategy, stage of internationalization, complexity of international operations, export sales percentage, export area, export sales per employee and size of the firm according to the number of employees. The firm's dependence on externally available resources is analysed by measuring two main indicators: (a) the firm's degree of domestic and foreign cooperation; and (b) the firm's degree of utilisation of other external sources (domestic and foreign) of information (Interstratos 1995). It has been argued that as the size of the firm increases, the level of activity in international operations also increases (Whitley 1980). However, how does the small firm's dependence on externally available resources change as the size of the firm increases or as the firm's degree of international orientation increases? Or can there be found different internationalization strategies for small firms concerning the use of external resources?

Specifically, this study considers the creation of empirically relevant propositions concerning the international orientation of the small firms and their dependence on externally available resources. This is done in order to more fully specify the relationships in focus for further study. The research setting consists of *Nordic (Finland, Sweden, Norway) small or medium-sized manufacturing companies* that had 1–500 employees. The sample includes two industries: *electronics and mechanical engineering industries* and jointly they are called the engineering firms. From the 690 engineering firms in the Nordic Interstratos (1993) data 238 firms with sufficiently complete data were selected for the analysis. All firms selected for the sample exported

Table 5.1 The sample (1993) of engineering firms from the Interstratos data

	Finland	Norway	Sweden
Electronics	19	18	46
Mechanical engineering	44	32	79

Size class distribution	(1–9)	(10–19)	(20–49)	(50–99)	(100–500)
Number of firms in each size class	12	41	50	52	83

their goods abroad and are, thus, internationally active firms. The purpose is not to claim that the firms selected are typical representatives of their industries but it is argued that they are good representatives of internationally active firms. A summary of the sample is shown in Table 5.1.

ACTIVITIES OF NORDIC ENGINEERING FIRMS

International activities

The international operations analysed include the following activities.

1 Buying foreign goods from local suppliers (stage 1)
2 Buying foreign goods from foreign suppliers (stage 1)
3 Manufacturing or selling under licence (stage 1)
4 Selling through an agent in the home country (stage 2)
5 Selling as supplier to an exporting producer (stage 2)
6 Selling to a local firm which eventually exports them (stage 2)
7 Selling through agents abroad (stage 2)
8 Selling directly to customers abroad (stage 3)
9 Licensing own products abroad (stage 3)
10 Having subsidiaries abroad for distribution (stage 4)
11 Having subsidiaries abroad for manufacturing (stage 5)

About 80 per cent of the firms buy foreign goods either/both from domestic and foreign sources. Direct exporting is used by over 80 per cent of the firms in the sample and 60 per cent of the firms use foreign agents in their exporting. The number of firms using indirect modes of exporting (about 20 per cent of firms) is lower than the number of firms using direct modes of exportation. This fact may be a reflection of the size class distribution of firms in the sample since the number of small firms (firms with less than fifty employees) is rather low compared to the number of medium-sized or bigger firms in the sample. Figure 5.1 shows these relationships.

The operations can be categorized also as stages of internationalization. A model of five stages was derived from the eleven modes of international operations: (1) inward stage; (2) indirect export stage; (3) direct export stage; (4) marketing unit investments abroad stage; and (5) manufacturing unit investments abroad stage. However, the behaviour of the firms cannot be analysed according to the stages directly, since the firms use simultaneously activities that can be classified into several categories. Thus the international strategy of the firms was measured by combining (a) the firm's stage of international development

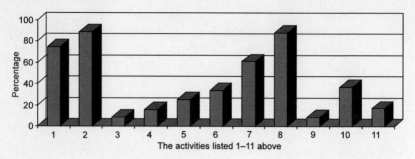

Figure 5.1 Frequency (%) of firms with international operations in the sample

that it has reached, and (b) the number of different simultaneously used international operations of the eleven mentioned above (complexity of export strategy). Since all the firms analysed have exportation, they all have already reached at least stage 2 in the development (7 per cent). More than half of the firms (53 per cent) represent stage 3 in the development and one fourth of the firms (24 per cent) are in stage 4 of the development. Only 16 per cent of the firms in the sample have made direct investments in manufacturing units abroad (stage 5). The complexity of export strategy varied between 1 and 10, the mean being 4.6 and standard deviation 1.7. The complexity of the export strategy was not found to have any relationship with firm size but a relationship was found between it and the stage of development, export area, and export sales percentage.

The area of export was classified into seven categories each of which represented a higher areal scope of operations. Scandinavia was the only export target for 12 per cent of the firms in the sample whereas 6 per cent of the firms exported to Europe but not to the other Nordic countries. For almost 40 per cent of the sample firms the area where the firm exports its goods includes Scandinavia and Europe and 20 per cent of the firms had already exported to Europe and some other area (either America or Asia). The last 20 per cent of firms had exports to at least three continents or they were acting globally. Figure 5.2 shows the cumulative frequency (percentage) of firms according to their scope of export area.

The percentage of export sales from total sales varied normally between 1 and 100 per cent. The mean for export sales percentage from total sales was 38 and standard deviation was 72 whereas the median was 30. The borderline between the first and second quartile was 10 and between the third and fourth quartile 64.

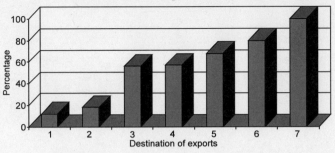

1 Scandinavia; 2 Europe (Scandinavia excluded); 3 Scandinavia and Europe; 4 Scandinavia and other areas outside Europe; 5 Europe (Scandinavia excluded) and other areas outside Europe; 6 Scandinavia, Europe, and one other area; 7 All Europe, America, and Asia or globally active

Figure 5.2 The (cumulative) frequency (%) of firms and the scope of export area

Domestic and foreign cooperation

Cooperation between firms is one of the means of achieving better (external) resources for internationalization. Firms can choose from a variety of activities in which they cooperate either in domestic or foreign markets. The following analysis focuses on cooperation either in *foreign* or *domestic* markets with both *domestic and foreign* partners. The analysed cooperation activities of firms were as follows.

 1 Extension of product range
 2 Research and development
 3 Raising funds
 4 Sales
 5 Marketing research
 6 After sales service
 7 Advertising/promotion
 8 Purchase/supply
 9 Transport/warehousing
10 Manufacture
11 Administration
12 Electronic data processing

Most frequent fields of domestic cooperation were sales (over 30 per cent of firms) and extensions of product range (27 per cent), but also R&D (almost 25 per cent) and manufacturing (over 20 per cent) were often mentioned by the engineering firms. Administration, after sales service, and raising funds were the least frequent fields of domestic cooperation in the sample. These results are to a great extent similar to the Interstratos (1995) results that are based on the total Interstratos data. The results are shown in Figure 5.3.

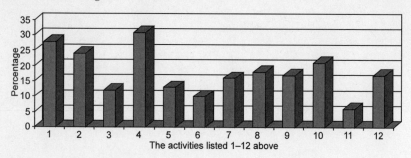

Figure 5.3 The frequency (%) of firms with domestic cooperation activities

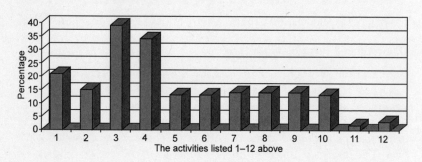

Figure 5.4 Frequencies (%) of firms with foreign cooperation activities

Foreign cooperation differs remarkably from domestic cooperation. The ranked importance of the different fields of cooperation is different as is their profile presented in Figure 5.4 compared to that of Figure 5.3. In foreign cooperation the most common fields of activity are raising funds (almost 40 per cent of firms) and sales (almost 35 per cent) whereas the importance of other fields of cooperation does not vary much. The lowest figures can be found in administration (2 per cent) and electronic data processing (3 per cent).

Utilization of domestic and foreign information sources

Firms may utilize a variety of different sources of information for internationalization both at home and in foreign markets. These included the following agencies.

1 Further training institutions
2 Consultants, etc.
3 Credit agencies
4 Suppliers

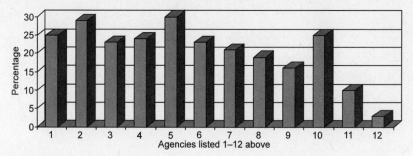

Figure 5.5 Frequency (%) of firms utilizing domestic information sources

5 Customers
6 Export clubs
7 Chamber of commerce
8 Research institutions
9 Public promotion fairs
10 National trade fairs
11 International trade fairs
12 International organizations

In the domestic markets the most often utilized sources of information included export clubs (30 per cent of firms), consultants (28 per cent), further training institutions (25 per cent), and customers (24 per cent). Least often information was acquired from international organizations (2 per cent) or from international trade fairs held in the home country (10 per cent). The percentage of firms utilizing other souces of information varied between 15 per cent (public promotion fairs) and 23 per cent (credit agencies). Figure 5.5 shows these findings.

In the foreign markets the number of firms utilizing the information sources was in general lower than in the domestic markets. But there is one source that is utilized more often abroad than at home: the international trade fair. Over 35 per cent of firms in the sample had attended international trade fairs in 1993. Also customers (30 per cent) were regarded as important sources of information. All other sources of information were of lower importance, at least firms were using them less often abroad than at home. Figure 5.6 shows these findings.

In summary, the international orientations among Nordic engineering firms are similar if the international activity profiles, export areas of the firms, and cooperation profiles are considered. However, the level of use of external information is high in Finland but low in Sweden. Also, there seem to be slight differences between the two industries in this respect (Interstratos 1995). However, the results

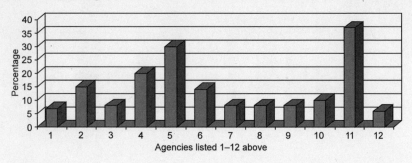

Figure 5.6 Frequency (%) of firms utilizing foreign information sources

presented here combine the results of both industries analysed – the electronics and mechanical engineering industries – since it is assumed that the overall international behaviour of the firms in the sample are rather homogenous.

INTERNATIONAL ORIENTATION AND DEPENDENCE ON EXTERNAL RESOURCES

In order to analyse the international orientation of the firms with regard to their external resource dependence several variables were created and used (summary in Table 5.2). The first class of variables in

Table 5.2 Variables and their operationalization, Interstratos

Variable	Operationalization
SIZE (size of the firm)	Number of employees
EXPO (export sales percentage)	(Export sales/total sales)*100
EMEX (export sales per employee)	Export sales per employee
STAG (stage of internationalization)	Stages (5) defined earlier, pp. 86–7
COMP (complexity of operations)	Number of simultaneously used international operations
STRA (internationalization strategy)	STAG + COMP
AREA (areal scope activities)	Areal scope or exporting (7) defined earlier in text,
DOCO (degree of domestic cooperation)	Number of simultaneously used domestic cooperation activities
FOCO (degree of foreign cooperation)	Number of simultaneously used foreign cooperation activities
DOIN (use of domestic information)	Number of simultaneously used domestic information sources
FOIN (use of foreign information)	Number of simultaneously used foreign information sources

Table 5.2 refers to the firm's size, export sales, export strategy (SIZE, EXPO, EMEX, STAG, COMP, STRA) and area of exportation (AREA). The second class of variables refers to the firm's domestic and foreign cooperation (DOCO, FOCO) and the third class of variables refers to the firm's use of externally available information (DOIN, FOIN). All the variables refer to the firm's strategic behaviour with respect to its internationalization although only the variables in the second and third class refer to the firm's degree of dependence on external resources.

In Table 5.3 the correlation matrix between the analysed variables is presented. Interestingly, in contrast to the assumption that as the size of the firm increases the level of activity in international operations increases, the size of the firm does not seem to correlate with the degree of cooperation nor with use of information for internationalization; only the use of information acquired from abroad correlates weakly (0.153) with the size of the firm. There is a low correlation between size and internationalization of the firm. Especially, in this respect size correlates with the scope of export area (0.236), with the stage of the firm (0.188), with export sales percentage (0.188), and with export strategy (0.135). There is quite strong correlation between export sales percentage, export sales per employee, and scope of export area. Also between the variables measuring the degree of cooperation and those measuring the degree of information use there can be found strong mutual correlations.

In order to study in a more detailed way the resource dependency of firms with regard to their internationalization, variables presented in Table 5.3 were standardized and factored (principal factor analysis), and the factor solution was then rotated (varimax). This resulted in a four factor model. The four factors accounted for 80 per cent of total variance in the sample. Each variable accounted only for one factor. In the first factor, orientation, the variables export sales percentage, export sales per employee and scope of export area were loaded heavily and this factor contributed 39 per cent of the total variation of the model. The factors, information use and cooperation, were also very clear, contributing 20 per cent and 12 per cent of the total variation, respectively. In the fourth factor, export strategy, were loaded the variables that referred to the firm's exportation stage and complexity. These factors are pure in the sense that the categories of variables are not mixed with each other. The model is displayed in Table 5.4

The main purpose of the factor analysis was to be able to classify the firms according to the factor loadings. From the performed K-Means cluster analyses (SPSS 6.1) a four cluster solution was selected.

Table 5.3 Means, standard deviations, Pearson's correlation coefficients and level of significance, N = 328

	Mean	Standard deviation	SIZE	EXPO	EMEX	AREA	STAG	COMP	STRA	DOCO	FOCO	DOIN	FOIN
SIZE	102.214	124.868	—										
p =													
EXPO	38.205	30.733	0.188	—									
p =			0.004										
EMEX	40.533	41.224	0.064	0.807	—								
p =			0.329	0.000									
AREA	4.105	2.028	0.236	0.560	0.452	—							
p =			0.000	0.000	0.000								
STAG	3.487	0.860	0.188	0.252	0.236	0.287	—						
p =			0.004	0.000	0.000	0.000							
COMP	4.639	1.683	0.086	0.238	0.218	0.277	0.536	—					
p =			0.188	0.000	0.001	0.000	0.000						
STRA	8.126	2.263	0.135	0.273	0.252	0.315	0.779	0.947	—				
p =			0.037	0.000	0.000	0.000	0.000	0.000					
DOCO	3.063	3.808	0.027	0.024	0.020	0.028	0.096	0.316	0.272	—			
p =			0.677	0.719	0.754	0.666	0.139	0.000	0.000				
FOCO	2.235	2.747	0.091	0.204	0.116	0.241	0.210	0.380	0.362	0.566	—		
p =			0.163	0.002	0.073	0.000	0.001	0.000	0.000	0.000			
DOIN	2.462	3.048	0.091	−0.039	−0.124	0.136	0.145	0.263	0.251	0.368	0.379	—	
p =			0.161	0.548	0.055	0.037	0.025	0.000	0.000	0.000	0.000		
FOIN	1.697	2.207	0.153	0.141	0.030	0.223	0.249	0.315	0.329	0.389	0.534	0.769	—
p =			0.018	0.029	0.646	0.001	0.000	0.000	0.000	0.000	0.000	0.000	
ORIE	118.730	82.504	0.185	0.828	0.818	0.546	0.351	0.419	0.444	0.301	0.427	0.340	0.494
p =			0.004	0.000	0.000	0.000	0.000	0.000	0.000	0.000	0.000	0.000	0.000

Table 5.4 Four-factor model of standardized variables

	Factor 1 orientation	Factor 2 information use	Factor 3 cooperation	Factor 4 export strategy
EXPO	0.934			
EMEX	0.905			
AREA	0.672			
DOIN		0.913		
FOIN		0.858		
DOCO			0.896	
FOCO			0.768	
STRA				0.948
COMP				0.851
STAG				0.829
SIZE				
Eigenvalue	5.42	2.78	1.61	1.41
Percentage	39	20	12	10

The four clusters comprised 93, 53, 52 and 40 firms, respectively. The variable profiles and the characteristics of the clusters are displayed in Figure 5.7, and Tables 5.5 and 5.6.

The first cluster (Cluster 1) with 93 firms was characterized by a simple exporting strategy as well as low cooperation, and low use of external information. A more detailed analysis of the clusters revealed interesting features of the firms. Cluster 1 included the smallest firms in the sample (mean of size 69) with low values in all variables but STAG (stage of internationalisation) for which the mean was 3 (direct exporting). Thus, the firms in Cluster 1 were underdeveloped compared to the other firms with regard to internationalization (the mean for export sales of total sales was 16 per cent and the mean for export sales per employee was 14,000 ECUs) and their degree of external

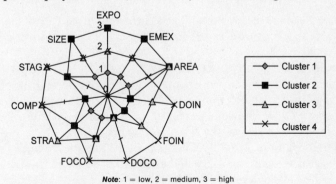

Note: 1 = low, 2 = medium, 3 = high

Figure 5.7 The variable profiles for clusters

Table 5.5 Cluster means and standard deviations

	Cluster 1		Cluster 2		Cluster 3		Cluster 4	
	Mean	*St. dev.*	*Mean*	*St. dev.*	*Mean*	*St. dev.*	*Mean*	*St. dev.*
EXPO	16	14	75	18	43	29	34	27
EMEX	14	12	91	43	42	32	33	31
AREA	3	2	5	2	5	2	4	2
DOIN	2	3	1	2	3	3	5	3
FOIN	1	1	1	2	3	3	4	3
DOCO	2	2	2	3	2	3	9	4
FOCO	1	1	2	2	2	2	6	3
STRA	7	1	8	2	11	2	9	2
COMP	4	1	4	1	6	2	6	2
STAG	3	1	3	1	4	1	4	1
SIZE	69	89	97	104	173	183	93	91

Table 5.6 Differences between cluster means (T-test)

	C1–C2	C1–C3	C1–C4	C2–C3	C2–C4	C3–C4
EXPO	+++	+++	+++	+++	+++	ns
EMEX	+++	+++	+++	+++	+++	ns
AREA	+++	+++	++	ns	+++	+
DOIN	ns	+++	+++	+++	+++	+
FOIN	ns	+++	+++	+++	+++	ns
DOCO	ns	ns	+++	ns	+++	+++
FOCO	+++	+++	+++	ns	+++	+++
STRA	+++	+++	+++	+++	+++	+++
COMP	++	+++	+++	+++	+++	ns
STAG	++	+++	+++	+++	+	+++
SIZE	ns	+++	ns	++	ns	++

Note: + significant at the level of 0.05, ++ significant at the level 0.01, +++ significant at the level 0.001, ns not significant

resource dependence was low. These firms might be called the 'starters' since their export area covered only Scandinavia and some European countries.

The second biggest cluster, Cluster 2, consisted of 53 firms with a high degree of international orientation measured by several internationalization variables, simple or focused export strategy (usually direct export), low use of external information but medium level of cooperation. The size of the firms in this cluster was 97 (mean) with standard deviation of 104. In Cluster 2 all the variables that were used to measure overall international orientation of the firm had high values. The mean for export sales percentage was 75 and the mean for export sales per employee was 91,000 ECUs in 1993. The usual export area for these firms were Europe and one other overseas area, e.g. America or Asia. The cooperation activities of the firms took place mainly in foreign markets. These firms might be called the 'advanced' since their scope of operations was well developed and their degree of international orientation was high.

Those 52 firms that fell into Cluster 3 were characterized by a medium level of general international orientation although their export strategy included a wide variety of different modes of exporting. These firms relied also on externally available information. The mean of the size of the firms was 173 which was the highest figure of all the clusters. The mean for export sales per total sales was 43 per cent and the exports per employee was 42,000 ECUs. The export area of the firms covered usually Europe and one other area outside it. The firms in this cluster operated approximately on an export area as large as the firms in Cluster 2. These firms had not been able to reach as high a degree of overall international orientation although they tried to rely more on externally available information both in domestic and foreign markets. The degree and profile of cooperation of the firms in Cluster 3 was the same as in Cluster 2. For these firms the export strategy used was quite complicated and, on average, consisted of a wide variety of different simultaneously used modes of exporting. The firms in this cluster might be characterized by the name 'learning' since they seemed to need more externally available information than the firms in the two previous clusters and their export strategy was rather complicated.

In Cluster 4 the firms were characterized by a high degree of external dependence and medium level of general international orientation. On average the export sales of total sales percentage was 34 and each employee was responsible for export sales of 33,000 ECUs in 1993. The export area of these firms was Europe including Scandinavia. The size of the firms in this cluster was approximately 93, with a standard deviation of 91. Interestingly these firms relied heavily on both domestic and foreign externally available information and cooperation, thus being highly dependent on external resources. It seems obvious that this kind of behaviour calls for a deliberate strategic decision to use external resources for internationalization. In summary, these firms might be called 'dependent'.

In Figure 5.8 below are presented the four clusters according to the four factors. The 'starters' (Cluster 1) were characterized by direct exports, a low degree of general international orientation and a low degree of external resource dependence. The 'learning' firms (Cluster 3) were characterized by medium levels of general international

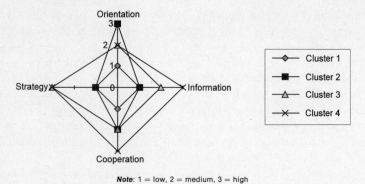

Figure 5.8 The factor profiles for clusters

orientation and medium levels of dependence on external resources. The 'dependent' firms (Cluster 4) were also characterized by medium levels of international orientation but a high degree of dependence on externally available resources. These firms relied heavily on both domestic and foreign information sources and they cooperated both in domestic and foreign markets in several fields of activity. The 'advanced' firms were highly internationalized with a focused export strategy but with a low degree of external resource dependence. However, these firms cooperated in foreign markets to an extent that can be characterized as medium if compared to the sample.

Table 5.7 displays the differences between cluster means according to the factors F1 (orientation), F2 (information use), F3 (cooperation) and F4 (export strategy).

Table 5.7 Differences between cluster means according to the factors (T-test)

	C1–C2	C1–C3	C1–C4	C2–C3	C2–C4	C3–C4
F1	+++	+++	++	+++	+++	ns
F2	ns	++	++	+++	+++	ns
F3	++	ns	+++	+	+++	+++
F4	ns	+++	+++	+++	+++	+++

Note: + significant at the level of 0.05, ++ significant at the level 0.01, +++ significant at the level 0.001, ns not significant

CONCLUSIONS

It has to be kept in mind that the methods used to measure external resource dependence are exploratory indicators of firm behaviour. Although the measures of internationalization have been widely used in the studies of internationalization, the indicators of external resource dependence, i.e. the domestic and foreign cooperation and information use, were aggregate measures referring to a variety of activities that firms may have and these activities have seldom been analysed with regard to internationalization. The reason why it is important to include domestic and foreign cooperation and information use when internationalization strategies and behaviour of firms is analysed is that internationalization can be regarded as development of firm resources through interaction within a network. In accordance with the learning-by-doing principle, which is often referred to in internationalization research (c.f. Johansson and Wiedersheim-Paul 1975), it is important to see firms in their environment; it is the environment that provides the resources for internationalization. This process may take place either through cooperative behaviour or through the use of other externally available resources, such as those studied here.

In addition, it has to be kept in mind that the data analysed here is a snapshot of the situation in which the firms were at one point of time (1993). Since internationalization is a process it should be studied longitudinally over time. However, cross sectional analyses can be used to produce classifications considering the firms' behaviour and other characteristics. The contribution of this kind of analysis to the process of internationalization is rather limited; these analyses do not tell us about the sequence nor logic of events, i.e. the process, in internationalization, but they may provide information about the possible international strategies the firms may have.

The size of the firm does not seem to explain internationalization nor the degree of dependence on externally available resources among Nordic engineering firms (Table 5.3). Even at best there can be found only low correlation between the firm's export strategy, its degree of international orientation, and size of the firm. Also, size does not correlate with the firm's degree of external resource dependence.

If the firm's degree of international orientation is studied against external resource dependence insightful results can be found. First, compared to the other engineering firms the advanced firms seem only to rely a little on the externally available resources. One hypothetical interpretation of this is that these firms have created some kind of advantage internally and they have used it as a driving force for internationalization. Thus, the advantage may have more potential in explaining the firm's behaviour than the possibly externally available resources. Of course, these firms also rely on external resources, especially through cooperation in foreign markets, but they do not cooperate in such a wide field of operations as the other learning and dependent firms. It also seems that the advanced firms operate according to the three rules established by Johansson and Mattsson (1988) that were discussed in the theory section.

The strategy of the learning and dependent firms does not seem to follow directly the theory formulated by Johansson and Mattsson (1988); these firms have recognized their need to *develop* knowledge and network positions in order to become more international. The key to this development seems to be the active and complex export strategy realized by these firms. What makes the difference between these two groups of firms is the degree to which they rely on external resources. The firms characterized as dependent rely heavily on external resources both through cooperation and through other information acquisition channels whereas the learning firms have a more focused strategy with regard to the external resources. It is especially the firm's cooperation behaviour that differentiates between these firms in this respect. It is conceivable that in these firms the advantage needed for internationalization is not as well developed as in the advanced group and thus they are forced to rely more on external resources. But, naturally, there may also be external reasons that contribute to this behaviour.

If the results are interpreted from the point of view of the starters, one of the most important factors is cooperation in foreign markets since it differentiates firms between Clusters 3 and 4, which might be the logical 'next steps' of the internationalization development. It also seems to be possible, according to the data, to decrease the firm's external information use as the firm's degree of internationalization increases but this is not the case with cooperation. In the sample the degree of cooperation does not decrease in any point of development as the firms become more international. Alas, this classification cannot tell much about how firms become more international; it just indicates that cooperation or some kind of internal advantage may result in internationalization or trigger it. It is the fact that if the export strategy of the firm is reflected against the firm's degree of international orientation it can be seen that the export strategy of the advanced and starter firms are similar; both relying on direct exports. The export strategy of the learning and dependent firms (with medium level of internationalization) includes the use of a much higher number of different exporting modes than the export strategy of the other groups. Indeed, there may be a connection between the export strategy and the firm's degree of dependency on external resources.

To summarize the results, the following conclusions might be drawn from the data of Nordic engineering firms that have international operations.

- Size of the firm does not tell much about the firm's degree of international orientation nor about the firm's degree of dependence on externally available resources.
- Internationally advanced firms – regardless of the size of the firm – rely more on internal resources than on externally available resources. In other words, as the firm's degree of international orientation increases its degree of dependence on externally available resources decreases. But, firms with a medium level of international orientation rely more on externally available resources than firms with a high or low degree of international orientation.
- With regard to internationalization and externally available resources, resource acquisition through cooperation is more important than the use of otherwise acquired resources.
- The export strategy (stage and complexity) of the firm is more complex among firms with a medium level of international orientation than among firms with a low or high degree of international orientation.

REFERENCES

Buckley, P.J. and Casson, M. (1976) *The Future of the Multinational Enterprise*, London: Macmillan.

Christensen, P. (1991) 'The small and medium-sized firms' squeeze: empirical evidence and model reflections', *Entrepreneurship & Regional Development*, 3: 49–65.

Conner, K. (1991) 'A historical comparison of resource-based theory and five schools of thought within industrial organisation economics: do we have a new theory of the firm?', *Journal of Management*, 17, 1: 121–54.

Czinkota, M.R. and Johnsson, W.J. (1981) 'Segmenting U.S. Firms for Export development', *Journal of Business Review*, 9:4, 353–65.

Gibb, A. and Scott, M. (1985) 'Strategic awareness, personal commitment, and the process of planning in small business', *Journal of Management Studies*, 22:6, 597–632.

Hurry, D. (1994) 'Shadow options and global exportation strategies', in P. Shrivastava, A. Huff and J. Dutton (eds) *Advances of Strategic Management*, vol. 10, Part A.

Interstratos (1995) 'Internationalization of strategic orientations of European small and medium enterprises', in A. Haahti (ed.), *EIASM Institute Report 95–01*, Brussels.

Johansson, J. and Mattsson, L. (1988) 'Internationalisation in industrial systems – a network approach', in H. Hood and J. Vahlne (eds) *Strategies in Global Competition* (eds), New York: Croom Helm.

Johansson, J. and Wiedersheim-Paul, F. (1975) 'The internationalization of the firm – four Swedish cases', *Journal of Management Studies,* 12:3, 305–22.

Luostarinen, R. and Hellman, H. (1993) 'Internationalization process and strategies of Finnish family enterprises', *Proceedings of The Conference on The Development and Strategies of SMEs in the 1990s,* 1: 17–35, Mikkeli.

Miesenböck, K.J. (1988) 'Small business and exporting: A literature review', *International Small Business Journal,* 6, 2: 42–58.

Norden i tal (1994) Utdrag ur Nordisk statistik årsbok 1994. Nordisk Ministerråd, Aka prints, Århus.

Nyström, H. (1990) *Technological and market innovation,* New York: Wiley.

Phatak, A. (1983) *International Dimensions of Management,* Belmont, CA: Wadsworth.

Rautkylä, R. (1991) 'Developing SME capabilities for the European Market', *Helsinki School of Economics Working Papers F262.*

Rugman, A. (1982) *New theories of the multinational enterprise,* London: Croom Helm.

Tallman, S., and Fladmoe-Lindquist, K. (1994) 'A resource-based model of the multinational firm', paper presented at the 1994 *Strategic Management Society Conference,* Paris.

Whitley, J. J. (1980) 'Differences between exporters and nonexporters: Some hypotheses concerning small manufacturing business', *American Journal of Small Business,* 4:3, 29–37.

6 Export orientation in open markets

The case of the Nordic countries[1]

Per-Anders Havnes, Johanne Sletten, and Arild Saether

INTRODUCTION

The process of opening the European markets which led to the establishment of the EU, has a less conspicuous and less known parallel in the open markets of the Nordic countries. As part of the EFTA agreement, there have been few restrictions and none or very low tariffs on trade of industrial products between Denmark, Finland, Sweden, and Norway since 1967. In the same period these countries have enjoyed a free labour market. Within these very open markets the industrial structures of Finland, Sweden and Norway have many similar features. Compared to the continental European countries, they also share low population density, and the population density of their northern regions is far below the national averages. Therefore, the manufacturing industries in these regions have small local markets combined with large distances to alternative markets. For many firms in the northern regions, the geographic distance to markets in neighbouring countries are shorter than to their domestic markets. This combination of extreme regional difference in market conditions and open foreign markets provide a unique opportunity for studying the effects of open markets.

In 1953 Chenery, Clark and Cao Pinna (1953) presented a study of the regional structure of the Italian economy. This study, which today is almost considered a classic, shows that the production and industrial structure of a region and its dependence on other regions for purchase of raw materials and semi-finished products and for the sale of their products can be a substantial hindrance to business growth and the equalization of income between regions. The indirect effects of an investment programme in southern Italy turned out to be greater in the north. The cause was the difference in industrial structure and southern Italy's dependence on the north for the purchase of semi-finished goods and for the export of its finished products.

This study initiated a whole range of studies entitled north-south or centre-periphery studies. It is neither the purpose of the present study to sum up the content of these earlier studies nor to give a critical appraisal of their theoretical basis. For our study it is enough to ascertain that the production and industrial structure of the northern areas of the three Nordic countries, called The North Calott, compared with the rest of these three countries has some of the same characteristics as between southern and northern Italy. Research studies of trade flows between the northern areas of the three Nordic countries, carried out by the University of Tromsø in 1977 and 1990 for The North Calott Committee supports this view (Nordkalottkomiteen 1977 and 1990).

The purpose of our investigation is to study, in an exploratory manner, how and to what extent firms of the North Calott have exploited the opportunities of open markets. In doing this we will study differences in industrial structures and ascertain if these are reflected in differences in export propensity, as one aspect of internationalization, between firms in northern and southern regions of these countries. As a background we will first give a short description of this region.

THE NORTH CALOTT

The North Calott is defined as the geographical area of the three Nordic countries laying wholly or partly north of the Polar Circle. This area consists of the five northernmost counties Nordland, Troms and Finnmark in Norway, Norrbotten in Sweden and Lappland in Finland. It is characterized by great distances, unfavourable natural and climatic conditions and a sparse population. However, it has also large forests, rich ore deposits, peat-bogs, water resources and huge wilderness areas with great possibilities for fishing, hunting and other tourist activities.

Table 6.1 The North Calott, area and population in 1990

Country	County	Area km²	Area %	Population 1990	Population per km²
Finland	Lappland	93,933	31.2	199,800	2.1
Norway	Finnmark	46,543	15.5	74,600	1.6
Norway	Troms	25,121	8.3	146,800	5.8
Norway	Nordland	36,288	12.1	239,400	6.6
Sweden	Norrbotten	98,906	32.9	262,800	2.7
Total	The North Calott	300,791	100.0	923,400	3.1

Source: The Statistical Yearbooks of the Nordic countries

From Table 6.1 it can be seen that the total area of The North Calott is a little more than 300,000 km². This is approximately one third of the total land area of the three Nordic countries and roughly the same area as Italy. At the end of 1990 the total population was only 923,000 or about 5 per cent of the total population of these three countries. It can also be seen that the population density on The North Calott is very low, 3.1 person per km² in 1990. Lappland county in Finland and Finnmark county in Norway are particularly sparsely populated.

From the turn of the century to 1960 there was a steady growth in the population in all of the five counties. The population increased from 455,000 in 1900 to 903,000 in 1960, i.e. almost a doubling. This growth was remarkably stronger than for the three countries as a whole. The reasons for this development were that the excess of births was higher than the average for the three countries and that the economic development in this period did not fall short of the rest of the three countries. In the 1960s and the 1970s the population still grew, but the growth rate was below the national averages. Over the past ten years the population has declined, mostly due to considerable migration.

Agriculture, forestry and fishing have traditionally employed a higher share of the economically active population in the northern areas than in the southern areas of the Nordic countries. Forestry has a very high share of employment in Lappland and Norrbotten, while agriculture has a high share of the employment in northern Norway. However, the importance of fisheries increases the further north we get in Norway.

The manufacturing enterprises in these northern areas are strongly linked to sectors which process local raw materials. Fish, agriculture, forestry and mining provide the raw materials for the greater part of the manufacturing industries. In the three Norwegian counties the manufacturing industry is dominated by food and beverages, in Finnish Lappland by wood, paper and pulp and in Swedish Norrbotten by iron and metals.

The share of population employed in the service sectors of the economy is almost the same in the northern and southern areas of the Nordic countries. However, the private service sector in the north has a lower share of the employed population and the public service sector a higher share.

The manufacturing industries employ a relatively lower share of the economic active population in the north than in the south. The manufacturing of metal products, machinery and equipment sector is of great importance on the North Calott. It is, however, strongly dependent on imported raw materials. This sector is also very different from one country to the other. Most of the enterprises in Lappland are engaged in machinery production. In northern Norway the main production is transport equipment and in Norrbotten metal products.

The above mentioned analysis of the trade flows (Nordkalottkomiteen 1977 and 1990) show that enterprises in the counties on the North Calott are heavily dependent on the southern part of the three countries. Such dependency need not in principle be negative. Strong linkages between two regions can have as a positive effect that growth in one region will spread to the other. This dependency has, however, for these northern areas, as for many other remote areas in other countries, a negative effect. Economic setbacks abroad or in the southern parts of the three countries have to a great extent been reflected in the northern areas. On the other hand, economic growth abroad or in the southern part has taken a long time to reach these areas and then they have been substantially weakened. This is a paradox considering the natural resources of these northern areas.

INTERNATIONALIZATION BEHAVIOUR

Over the past ten to fifteen years several studies have been carried out with the purpose of studying the internationalization process and the export behaviour of enterprises (Gripsrud 1990; Andersen 1991 and 1993). Researchers who study the internationalization process of small and medium sized enterprises face considerable problems. In the first place the research based knowledge about internationalization is fragmented. We do not have what can be called a general theory, understood as providing generally valid explanations. Second, we do not have a uniform theory of the behaviour of small and medium-sized enterprises.

Although several extensive and interesting studies discuss the export behaviour of small and medium-sized firms, the lack of a theoretical superstructure implies that the 'findings' must be seen in the context of the particular investigation which often varies with respect to the problem, definitions of concepts, types of firms and industry sectors.

There are many different approaches to studies of internationalization, but one element seems to receive wide support. The internationalization is often seen as a gradual process (Johanson and Vahlne 1977; Cavusgil 1984; Welch and Luostarinen 1988; 1990; Andersen 1991 and 1993), where firms will gradually adapt to an international market through a sequence of stages and this process also holds for the small and medium-sized enterprises. Furthermore, firms will enter new foreign markets with successively greater psychic distance. The latter concept has been defined as factors preventing or disturbing the flow of information between firms and markets including factors such as differences in language, culture, political systems, level of education, or level of industrial development. (Johanson and Vahlne 1977).

Empirical studies, reviewed by Andersen (1991), indicate that the content and outcome of the internationalization process to a large extent is determined by the firms' internal and external environments, how the firms react to export stimuli and the qualities of the decision maker. These factors have also been used to map the differences between exporters and non-exporters or very active and less active exporters.

Andersen (1991), in his empirical study, focused on the differences in export activity and in the internationalization process among Norwegian enterprises in mechanical industries located in central and peripheral areas, that is southern and northern Norway. In addition he tested whether there is a difference between the size of the national market and export activity among enterprises in the same areas. He found that the share of mechanical enterprises which export is three times higher in central areas than in the periphery. His data from 1981 and 1986 also showed that the difference declined over time. The differences in size of the enterprises could not explain this difference, although there is a weak correlation between export share and size.

His results support the hypothesis that enterprises pass through a form of 'internationalization process' on the home market before they are ready for the export market. It appears as if enterprises in the periphery have greater problems in obtaining a national market.

There may be several possible reasons for a higher share of export activities among centrally located enterprises compared to corresponding enterprises located in the periphery. First, enterprises in the periphery can have a management and key personnel with lower levels of education or they may lack personnel with qualifications in international marketing. According to Andersen (1991) the educational level was lower in enterprises located in peripheral areas. Another point is that enterprises on the periphery are exposed to a lesser degree to external stimuli towards exporting – unsolicited orders, governmental export drives or pressure from other exporting businesses in the local community – since there are few which export.

METHODOLOGY

Exploratory model

The purpose of the present study is to investigate possible relationships between the location of firms and their export propensity. The analytical approach of the study is explorative. The exploratory approach requires an open mind to possible and probable but also unexpected relationships.

The fact that we are exploring a data set which was originally not designed for the purpose focused upon in this paper, puts some practical restraints on the design of the model, which necessitates some compromises.

The initial question raised in this chapter can be rephrased to: Is there any relationship between the location of a firm and its export propensity?

There are only a few possible direct effects between these two concepts; one example is local resources in excess of national demand, another is the existing transportation facilities. However, there are also a number of potential intervening variables of varying complexity. Of these we have chosen to focus on the following:

- Firm characteristics, with the components size and industry sector.
- Management characteristics, with the components education, experience in industry, language skills, time spent abroad and attitudes.
- Market contact, with the components marketing activity level, regularity of receiving orders and marketing channels.
- Market distance, with the components local sale and export countries.

These concepts coincide or correspond with concepts used in several other studies of export performance of SMEs (see, amongst others, Kanyak and Ghauri 1987; Schlegelmilch and Crook 1988; Culpan 1989; Sriram and Sapienza 1991; Bonaccorsi 1992; Andersen 1991 and 1993; and Manchini and Prince 1993). However, none of these uses the same constellation of concepts as presented in our model.

We are interested in the importance of the direct effects between location and export propensity as well as the indirect effects through the intervening variables. Our objective is to test what we consider the most likely of these relationships. At this stage, we will not try to reduce the number of variables through factor analysis or to make any multivariate tests. Our research objectives are reached through univariate tests on the individual relationships. The concepts we are going to use and the relationships to be tested are depicted in Figure 6.1.

There is a potential two way relationship between all of these variables. As we are not attempting to test hypotheses of causal relationships, there is no need to test for direction of relationships.

The main benefits of this approach are that it provides direct evidence of relationships and a clear over-all view. The statistical tests can also be handled and interpreted easily. The main disadvantages

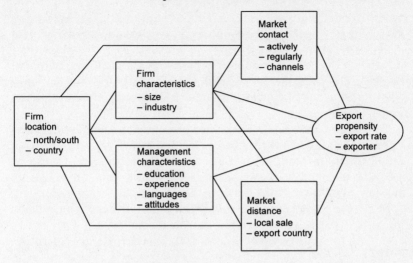

Figure 6.1 Relationship between firm location and export propensity

are that we do not test for complex relationships of feed-back mechanisms. A further disadvantage is that using one dimensional variables might be insufficient to discriminate between effects related to exporting (Manchini and Prince 1993). However, as the purpose at this stage is mainly to explore the data, the benefits outweigh the disadvantages. Bearing in mind the acknowledged limitations of our testing procedures, one must be cautious not to draw too strong conclusions based on the results.

DATA

The Interstratos project is described in Chapter 1. Our study uses the data set from the 1992 study in Finland, Sweden and Norway; which includes 1,404 enterprises. The distribution of these firms by country and region is shown in Table 6.2.

Table 6.2 Sample: number of enterprises by country and region

	Firms from							
	Finland		Norway		Sweden		Total	
	North	South	North	South	North	South	North	South
N (firms)	6	363	27	321	20	667	53	1351
North/south % (firms)	1.6	98.4	7.8	92.2	2.9	97.1	3.8	94.2

The North Calott as a whole has almost 4 per cent of the enterprises in the sample from the three countries. If we look at the distribution of enterprises between the northern and southern part of each country we see that the northern counties in Norway have almost 8 per cent of the enterprises in the Norwegian sample while the northernmost county in Finland, Lappland has only 1.6 per cent of the enterprises in the Finnish sample.

Tables 6.A1 and 6.A2 of the appendix show the number of enterprises in the sample, distributed by size classes and industry sectors in the northern and southern regions. From these two tables it can be seen that the number of enterprises in the two smallest size groups are substantially higher in the north than in the south.

More than 58 per cent of the enterprises in the north are to be found in these two groups against 41 per cent in the south. The distribution according to industry sectors shows that 32 per cent of all enterprises in the north are found in the food, beverages and tobacco industry compared to 18 per cent in the south. On the other hand, the share of the number of enterprises in the industry sectors, textiles and electronics, is substantially lower in the north than in the south. The sample is reasonably representative of the real distribution of enterprises among the five manufacturing sectors between the northern and southern regions of the three Nordic countries.

Because of the small number of enterprises in the sample from the northern areas of the three countries it has been necessary for the statistical tests to regroup the enterprises according to size classes and industry sectors. For the three northernmost counties of Norway the firms have been regrouped into two industry sectors. Food, beverages and tobacco is kept as one sector but the four other manufacturing sectors in our sample have been aggregated into one sector. For the northernmost county of Sweden, Norrbotten, the firms have also been regrouped into two industry sectors. Mechanical industry is kept as one sector but the four other manufacturing sectors have been aggregated into one sector.

For the northernmost county of Finland, Lappland, the sample contains only firms in two manufacturing sectors. Food, beverages and tobacco is one sector and the other sector is mechanical engineering.

It has also been necessary to regroup the size classes. For the northernmost counties of Norway and the northernmost county of Sweden the five size groups have been regrouped into three size classes; 1–19, 20–49 and 50–499 employees. In Finnish Lappland only two size classes are represented, that is 10–19 and 20–49 employees.

ANALYSIS

This part examines the relationships in our model. One important feature will be to evaluate the effects of the intervening variables. In order to accept that an intervening variable has a potential role in the model, we require that it shall be part of an unbroken chain of significant relationships between the independent variable 'firm location' and the dependent variable 'export propensity'.

Statistical tests

For relationships between nominal variables the statistical significance has been tested by Pearson's χ^2 test. Relationships between nominal and interval variables have been tested by analysis of variance.

All results have been controlled for the effects of firm size and industry sectors. The effects of location have been controlled for in three ways where appropriate:

- differences between north and south within each country;
- differences between the north/south patterns of each of the three countries; and
- differences between the total distributions for the three countries.

In this way we may discriminate between location effects intrinsic to one specific country and location effects of a more general nature.

The level of significance has been set at 0.05 in the present study.

Firm location and export propensity

The export propensity has two measures:

- exporter, with the values 'yes', 'no' and 'missing'; and
- export rate, where the value of export sales is given as a percentage of the total sales.

Exporter

As shown in Table 6.3, the percentage of exporting firms is significantly lower in the northern region of Norway than in the southern region. The same pattern is found in the two other countries. However, the differences between north and south are not statistically significant in these countries. The main differences between the countries are that the number of exporters is higher in Sweden than in the two other countries and that there is more difference between north and south in Norway than in the two other countries.

Table 6.3 Location related to differences in number of exporters, % of firms

| | Firms from | | | | | |
| | Finland | | Norway | | Sweden | |
	North	South	North	South	North	South
Region						
% exporters	67	75	48	76	70	80
N (firms)	6	348	27	321	20	667
Statistical significance	–		+		–	
Country						
% exporters	75		74		79	
Statistical significance			+			

Export rate

When using the export rate (export sales as a percentage of total sales) of the exporting firms to measure export propensity, we find no pattern similar to that found for the exporter/non-exporter measure. There is no significant difference in the export rates, neither between north and south within each country, nor between the countries. These results are shown in Table 6.4.

Control for industry sectors and firm size

When the relative number of exporters are controlled for industries there are obvious differences in the number of exporting firms within different industries. The food industry tends to be domestic oriented, with a low percentage of exporters. The mechanical industry tends to have a high number of exporters. This picture is somewhat blurred

Table 6.4 Location related differences in export rates, exports as % of total sales

| | Firms from | | | | | |
| | Finland | | Norway | | Sweden | |
	North	South	North	South	North	South
Region						
Average export rate	36	31	31	31	35	27
N (firms)	2	170	13	155	10	667
Statistical significance	–		–		–	
Country						
Average export rate	31		31		28	
Statistical significance			–			

when the regions are analysed individually, partly because samples from the three northern regions differ as to the distribution of industries.

When the regional analyses of exporters are controlled for size of firms, some very interesting results appear. As expected from results from other research, the relative number of exporters increase by increasing size of firms in north and south of all three countries. But there is more difference between north and south for the smallest firms than for the largest. For the largest firms the location factor has negligible effect on the measure 'exporter/non-exporter'. This effect is uniform for all three countries.

There is no apparent pattern between north and south when similar controls are made for the variable 'export rate'. The relationship between export rates and size seems to differ, and the patterns are different in the three countries. But it is interesting to find that the food industry, with a low relative number of exporters, has high average export rates in Norway compared to the other industries. More so in the northern region than in the south. This points to the importance of the local resource of fish as the main basis for the exporting industries. The Finnish food industry in the north, although few firms in number, also has high export rates, while the same industry in the south has low export rates. The results from Sweden are ambiguous.

Firm location and management characteristics

As discussed above, the educational level, industry experience and knowledge of languages and foreign culture of the management in SMEs are expected to influence the internationalization process of the enterprises. The management's attitudes towards government interference, planning, etc. are also expected to be reflected in how the enterprises develop.

The Interstratos questionnaire has several questions related to the management's background and attitudes. This analysis concentrates on the questions of age of managers when they finished their education, numbers of years of experience in the industry, numbers of spoken languages (including mother languages) and numbers of weeks spent abroad during the last three years.

Managers' education and experience

We find no significant differences between north and south in each country regarding these management characteristics. This is in contrast

Table 6.5 Management characteristics

| | Firms from | | | | | |
| | Finland | | Norway | | Sweden | |
	North	South	North	South	North	South
Average age when finished education	23	23	26	24	23	23
Average years of industry experience	18	18	15	17	20	21
Languages spoken[1]	2.0	3.0	2.5	2.8	2.6	2.7
Weeks abroad last three years	11	12	11	9	8	11
N (firms)	6	329	27	321	20	670
Statistical significance	–		–		–	

Note: [1] Including mother tongue

with Andersen's (1991) observations. The results are summarized in Table 6.5.

We have also checked each of the characteristic variables for differences between exporters and non-exporters and between different industries and size-classes. We find no such difference to be significant, except for numbers of years of experience in industry between exporters and non-exporters in Norway. In Norway, the managers of exporting enterprises have an average of 17 years of experience in the industry, while the number for managers of non-exporting enterprises is 14. The difference is even more obvious when comparing just the enterprises located in the north of Norway. In this area the average number of years of experience for managers of exporting enterprises is 19 and for managers of non-exporting companies 11 years.

Managers' attitudes

In the Interstratos questionnaire the managers were asked to evaluate statements regarding attitudes towards government and private organizations, willingness to accept change, planning and administration, reluctance to change, personal image and attitudes towards employees and the relations between business and family life. To reveal the managers' attitudes, they were asked to indicate to what degree they agreed with the statements on a scale from 1 'very much disagree' to 5 'very much agree'.

We find significant differences between north and south for only a few of the statements and only in Sweden and Finland. However, the number of Finnish enterprises in the north are so limited that we cannot draw any conclusion. For the Swedish enterprises the results show that the managers of enterprises located in the north disagree more with the statements 'the entrepreneur should plan rather than follow intuition' and in family owned businesses 'the management should stay in the hands of the family' than the enterprises in the south. The managers of enterprises in the north of Sweden are also significantly more positive to the statement 'SMEs should not hesitate to do business with large firms'. Table 6.6 shows these findings clearly.

Table 6.6 Attitude statements, average scores

	Finland		Firms from Norway		Sweden	
	North	South	North	South	North	South
Government should not restrict markets, not even through use of incentives	3.8	3.8	3.2#	3.3#	3.5	3.6
Professional bodies and similar organizations should only assist members	3.3	3.5	3.5	3.2	3.7	3.8
Changes should be avoided at all cost	2.1	1.7	1.4	1.5	1.1	1.3
Firms should not leave the region	2.3	1.9	2.7#	2.5#	1.8	2.0
Working tasks should be planned in detail	2.6	2.6	3.6	3.3	2.6	3.0
The entrepreneur should plan rather than follow intuition	2.8	3.0	3.6	3.5	2.1*	2.5*
Firms should only introduce proven office procedures and production techniques	2.5	2.8	2.7	2.7	2.2	2.3
In family owned businesses the management should stay in the hands of the family	2.3	2.7	2.2#	2.2#	1.9*	2.7*
Small firms should not hesitate to do business with large firms	4.2	4.2	3.7	3.5	4.9*	4.3*
SME managers should take personal responsibility for recruiting employees	2.8	3.2	3.6	3.5	4.0	3.7
A manager should consider ethical principles in his behaviour	3.0*	3.9*	3.9	4.0	3.6	3.7
Business should take precedence over family life	2.2	2.4	2.4	2.4	2.3	2.6
N (firms)	6	343	26	304	20	646

Notes: 1 = very much disagree, 5 = very much agree
* significant differences between north and south
# significantly different from the other countries

We find significant differences between the countries for several of the statements. Norwegian enterprises are significantly less negative to government interference than the Swedish and Finnish enterprises. We also find that the Norwegian enterprises are significantly less interested in moving out of the region where they are located today than enterprises in the two other countries. Norwegian enterprises are, on the other hand, significantly more positive to including non-family members in the management of family owned enterprises.

However, one should be careful and not draw far reaching conclusions at this stage since other factors, such as national related interpretations of the scale, may have strong influence on the responses to attitude questions (Blais and Toulouse 1990).

When examining the questions presented in Table 6.6 for differences between exporters and non-exporters we find significant differences for three statements only. Exporting firms are more positive to moving out of the region where they are located. They are also more in favour of planning. Non-exporting firms, on the other hand, are more positive towards including non-family in the management of family owned firms.

MARKET CONTACT

Firm location and market contact

The firms' market contact can be evaluated based on their level of marketing activity and regularity of receiving orders. In the Interstratos questionnaire the firms were asked whether they are marketing actively on the export market or not, and if they are receiving export orders regularly or not. Table 6.7 shows the results on marketing activity.

Table 6.7 Export market contact measured by activity level of marketing, % of firms

| | Firms from | | | | | |
| | Finland | | Norway | | Sweden | |
	North	South	North	South	North	South
Region						
% actively marketing	0	40	33	42	35	35
N (firms)	5	237	21	221	17	671
Statistical significance	–		–		–	
Country						
% actively marketing	40		41		35	
Statistical significance			–			

Between 30 and 40 per cent of the companies claim to be actively marketing their products on their export markets. We find no significant differences when comparing the Nordic countries. Nor do we find significant differences when controlling for the north/south dimension. We have also controlled for differences related to industry sector and size-class, but no obvious pattern was found.

The second aspect of market contact is the regularity of receiving export orders. A firm that receives export orders regularly, will have frequent direct interchange of information with the foreign market.

There are no significant differences between north and south within any of the Nordic countries. However, there are significant differences between the countries regarding regularity of receiving export orders. Almost 50 per cent of the Swedish firms receive export orders regularly, independent of location, while the number is below 30 per cent for both Norway and Finland. When controlled for firm size the same, and expected tendency, is found in the southern regions of all three countries: the percentage of exporters receiving orders regularly increases with growing firm size. The same tendency is not found in the northern regions in our sample. One reason for that may be the few observations in these regions. Table 6.8 summarizes these findings on the receipt of export orders.

Market contact and export propensity

These relationships must be tested with the export rate as dependent variable, the reason being that non-exporters have no export market

Table 6.8 Export market contact measured by regularity of receiving export orders, % of firms

| | Firms from | | | | | |
| | Finland | | Norway | | Sweden | |
	North	South	North	South	North	South
Region						
% receiving export orders regularly	–	29	24	30	40	47
N (firms)	4	259	21	221	18	658
Statistical significance	–		–		–	
Country						
% receiving export orders regularly	29		30		47	
Statistical significance			+			

Table 6.9 Activity of marketing and export rate in % of total sales

	Finland		Firms from Norway		Sweden	
	North	South	North	South	North	South
Region						
Actively marketing	–	33	35	23	18	25
Not actively marketing	36	27	33	28	46	29
N (firms)	2	115	11	111	10	294
Statistical significance	–		–		–	
Country						
Actively marketing		36		34		24
Not actively marketing		30		27		29
Statistical significance				–		

to contact. The effects of contact with potential export customers will not be visible until later. The relationships are tested by comparing mean export rates for exporters related to active marketing and regularity of receiving export orders. The findings on export rates are shown in Table 6.9.

It might, perhaps, seem surprising that the actively marketing firms in many situations have lower average export rates than the firms which are not actively marketing. It should be sufficient to be reminded that the potential causal effect between these two concepts is bi-directional. The firm may wish to improve a poor export performance through active marketing, or it may have a high export rate because it is and has been marketing actively. Table 6.10 displays the findings here.

Table 6.10 Regularity of receiving export orders and export rate in % of total sales

	Finland		Firms from Norway		Sweden	
	North	South	North	South	North	South
Region						
Receiving orders regularly	–	26	40	41	30	26
Not receiving orders regularly	62	31	26	28	38	29
N (firms)	1	126	9	106	10	301
Statistical significance	–		–		–	
Country						
Receiving orders regularly		26		41		27
Not receiving orders regularly		31		28		29
Statistical significance		–		–		–

Exporting channels

The Interstratos questionnaire has several questions related to the mode of contact with foreign customers. In this context we have regrouped the responses and identified two main exporting channels:

- sales through a domestic intermediary; and
- sales directly to a foreign customer or intermediary.

The main difference between these two modes is that the second requires that the firm is able to establish and maintain direct contact with foreign companies. In maintaining the direct contact the firm will also gain a source of information from the foreign market. These characteristics are shown in Table 6.11.

The number of Finnish firms in the northern region is too small to make statistical tests meaningful for this country. Also a large number of the Swedish firms seems to have exporting channels which did not correspond with the questionnaire.

However, when seeing the results of Tables 6.9, 6.10 and 6.11 in combination we find no support for assuming that there is a consistent north/south difference in marketing methods or the selection of exporting channels. In other words, regional differences in export propensity are not likely to be caused by regional (north/south) differences in the market contact of exporting firms or selection of distribution channels.

These results are controlled for the effects of industries and size for each country separately. Industry sectors do not seem to have any statistical effect. In Norway the smallest firms seem to favour domestic channels while the larger firms favour foreign channels. However, these differences are not repeated for the two other countries. For the three countries as a group, firm size has no significant influence on exporting channels.

Table 6.11 Exporting channels, % of firms

| | Firms from | | | | | |
| | Finland | | Norway | | Sweden | |
	North	South	North	South	North	South
Domestic only	0	17	15	15	0	0
Domestic and foreign	0	28	23	36	7	1
Foreign only	50	24	39	22	21	22
Others	50	31	23	27	72	77
N (firms)	4	260	13	244	14	534
Statistical significance		–		–		–

MARKET DISTANCE

Firm location and market distance

One common dimension for the northern regions of the three Nordic countries is low density of population, and hence small local markets. This may have two effects: the firms may seek other markets at home or abroad; or the local markets may define the limits to growth for each firm.

Another important dimension is that the geographic distances to markets are large and local distribution systems are weak. The geographic distance to the neighbouring countries are often smaller than to the large domestic markets, and definitely smaller than to other export markets.

The potential effects of market distance are examined by analysing the local sales and export markets of firms with different locations with special attention to exports to neighbouring countries.

Local sale

Local sale is defined as the percentage of total sales within a radius of 50 km of the manufacturing firm. The regional and national differences in local sale are presented in Table 6.12. Although the low number of firms in the northern regions has a negative effect on the statistical validity of the test, the tendency in the results is the same for all three countries. There is more focus on local markets in the north than in the south.

When the northern and southern regions of all three countries are seen as two groups, we find that the proportion of local sale is significantly higher, 37 per cent in the north versus only 25 per cent in

Table 6.12 Regional differences in sales to local markets, % of total sales

| | By firms from | | | | | |
| | Finland | | Norway | | Sweden | |
	North	South	North	South	North	South
Region						
average	55	28	32	25	39	23
N (firms)	6	351	27	321	20	670
Statistical significance	–		–		+	
Country average	29		26		23	
Statistical significance			+			

the south. The results havè been controlled for the effects of industry sector and firm size. These two factors offer no explanation for the differences between north and south in either of the countries.

Export markets

The psychic distance between northern Norway and northern Sweden is very small along most dimensions while there is a language barrier between Finland and the other Nordic countries. However, this barrier exists between Finland and all countries. For the other dimensions of psychic distance, Norway and Sweden are very close to Finland. The geographic distances between these countries are smaller than in any other export market.

One measure of the relative importance of different export markets is the frequency of each country being mentioned as an export market. Table 6.13 uses this measure to define the important markets for the Nordic firms. The table shows that 33 per cent of all the exporting firms in the northern region of Finland mention Norway as an export market, etc.

The firms in northern Finland and Norway seem to be more focused on the Nordic market than their colleagues in the south. This tendency is reversed in Sweden. However, we have a low number of observations in our sample, especially for Finland, and the observed differences are therefore not statistically significant.

Another measure of the export market is available in the Interstratos data set. This is the 'most important export market' for the firms (see appendix 1). The neighbouring countries and Germany are important export markets for all the Nordic countries, but like the previous measure this test gives no support for an assumption that there might be more trade with the neighbouring countries in the north as compared with firms in the south. Table 6.A3 of the appendix also suggests that when the observations include few cases, factors other than distance play an important role. In other words, on a

Table 6.13 Frequency of Nordic export markets, percentage of firms

| | Exporting by firms from | | | | | |
| | Finland | | Norway | | Sweden | |
Export market	North	South	North	South	North	South
Finland	–	–	13	6	15	29
Norway	33	22	–	–	20	40
Sweden	33	41	38	26	–	–

macro scale where firms from the whole country are included, there seems to be a certain support for the 'psychic distance' paradigm. However, the same observation may be attributed to the existence of the Nordic open market. Whatever the reason, Nordic countries trade with each other more than with other countries. When few firms are included, other factors seem to override the effect of this mechanism.

Market distance and export propensity

Our model utilizes one set of measures from the Interstratos data for the relationship between market distance and export propensity – the relationship between the variables 'local market sale' and 'exporters/ non-exporters'. This part of the model is therefore tested by establishing possible relationships between the extent of the local market sales and exporters/non-exporters (see Table 6.14). The results are ambiguous as to the relationships between local market sales and exporting.

When the results in Table 6.14 are controlled for regional effects, we find that the differences between the countries go beyond the averages. There are also structural differences in the relationships between local sales and export sales:

- In northern Finland both exporters and non-exporters have high and not very different local sales (57 per cent and 50 per cent). However, this group consists of only seven firms. In the south there is no difference between exporters and non-exporters (29 per cent).
- In northern Norway the exporters have a very low proportion of local sales (13 per cent) while the non-exporters have a high proportion of local sales (49 per cent). Thus, the non-exporters contribute to the high level of local sales in northern Norway. In the south exporters also tend to have lower local sales (24 per cent) than non-exporters (29 per cent), but the difference here is smaller.

Table 6.14 Exporters and sales to local markets, % of total sales

| | Finland | | By firms from Norway | | Sweden | |
	Exporter	Non-exporter	Exporter	Non-exporter	Exporter	Non-exporter
Country average	29	29	23	32	24	20
N (firms)	277	92	257	91	548	139
Statistical significance	–		+		–	

- The Swedish firms display the third pattern; lower local sale for exporters in the north (34 per cent) than for non-exporters (52 per cent). In the south the exporters have the highest proportion of local sales (24 per cent) while the non-exporters have 18 percent.

In other words, local sales and export sales are equally important for firms in the south and north of Finland. In Norway there seems to be a group of exporters in the north where local sales are of low importance, while the non-exporters have almost as much focus on local sale as the firms in northern Finland. In southern Norway the local sales are of less importance and again less important for exporters than non-exporters. The exporters of southern Sweden break this pattern with higher emphasis on local sales than the non-exporters.

DISCUSSION OF RESULTS

The acknowledged consequence of using simple testing procedures prevents us from drawing firm conclusions at this stage. However, the results open up some interesting observations and interpretations, which may be further tested in another setting. The findings discussed on the previous pages are summarized in Figure 6.2 where bold lines, boxes and texts indicate statistically significant relationships.

We have found direct as well as indirect relationships between firm location and export propensity, but only when export propensity is measured by the variable 'exporter/non-exporter'. The export rates of firms that are exporters do not vary with the location of the firms. The

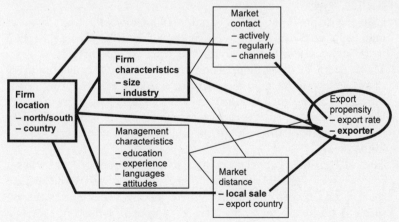

Figure 6.2 Significant relationships between firm location and export propensity

most important intervening factor is 'firm characteristics', that is the firms' size and industry sectors. A large part of the differences between northern and southern regions may be attributed to these factors. With one exception there is no other unbroken chain of relationships between location and export propensity. This exception is sales to the local market, which varies with geographic location and covaries with the variable 'exporter/non-exporter'. However, we have found no apparent pattern in these relationships.

Our observed variations along the geographic dimension can be summed up in the following interesting features:

- There is a difference between firms in the north and in the south when it comes to the percentage of firms which are exporters. There are more exporters in the south than in the north, even when controlled for industry sector. Further, this difference decreases consistently with growing size of the firm. This observation is the same for all three countries. There are also differences between the countries as to the percentage of the firms that are exporters. However, these differences are smaller than the regional differences within each country.
- There is no similar consistency for the export rate of the exporting firms.
- Export propensity is related to the industry sectors in the countries. The food and beverage industry is an example of an industry with few exporters. Mechanical engineering is an example of an industry with a high number of exporters. These findings coincide with other studies.
- Other possible intervening variables which were tested, such as management characteristics and market contacts, did not discriminate between firms in the south and firms in the north.
- There is no evidence supporting the view that the neighbouring countries are more important export markets for the firms in the northern regions than for the firms in the south. This coincides with other studies. However, trade with neighbouring countries is very important for all three countries, which supports the psychic distance theory.
- The relationships between export rate and the rate of local market sales suggest a possible connection between the strength of the local market and export propensity. Where the local market is weak we seem to find exporters who focus on the export market, that is a high export rate. Where the local market is strong the exporters

have a tendency for dividing their focus more between domestic and foreign markets.

● The attitude variables did not, generally, discriminate between managers from the northern and southern regions. Our findings give no support for assuming that these attitude variables contribute to the differences of export propensity.

The perspective of the open Nordic markets gives room for two interesting observations. On a national level we found that trade with the neighbouring countries is more important than the size of their respective economies would indicate. This could potentially be explained by transportation costs, by the psychic distance theory, or by the effects of the open Nordic markets. If the first two reasons were dominant, we should expect the inter-Nordic trade to be even more important in the northern regions than in the south because the markets of the North Calott are closer to each other than to any other market. The lack of difference between north and south regarding inter-Nordic trade, suggests that the open market is very important for the stimulation of exports.

The second observation is that there are many structural differences between the industries of the three countries. These differences relate to industry sectors, export propensity, local sales, relative differences between northern and southern regions within the same country, etc. – in other words to a variety of dimensions. Observing these differences after almost thirty years of open markets underlines that market accessibility is only one of many factors that influence industrial development.

APPENDIX

Table 6.A1 Distribution of firms in northern regions, all three countries, number of firms

		Firm size (employees)				Sum N	%
	1–9	10–19	20–49	50–99	100–499		
TEXT	1	1	1	1	–	4	8
ELEC	1	3	3	1	1	5	9
FOOD	8	3	2	3	2	17	32
WOOD	3	2	5	–	1	8	15
MECH	3	6	–	–	2	19	36
Sum	16	15	11	5	6	53	
%	30	28	21	10	11		100

Table 6.A2 Distribution of firms in southern regions, all three countries, number of firms

| | Firm size (employees) | | | | | Sum N | % |
	1–9	*10–19*	*20–49*	*50–99*	*100–499*		
TEXT	54	52	64	24	30	224	17
ELEC	61	52	69	29	29	240	18
FOOD	39	60	50	41	55	245	18
WOOD	56	47	67	24	24	218	16
MECH	63	73	92	94	92	414	31
Sum	273	284	342	212	230	1,341	
%	20	21	26	16	17		100

Table 6.A3 Frequency mentioned as 'most important export market'

| | Exporting firms from | | | | | |
| | Finland | | Norway | | Sweden | |
Export market	*North*	*South*	*North*	*South*	*North*	*South*
Germany	50	14	14	17	–	19
UK	–	4	–	7	10	6
Turkey	–	–	14	–	–	–
Italy	–	–	–	2	10	1
Denmark	–	2	14	11	20	9
Norway	–	9	*	*	20	30
Sweden	50	47	14	42	*	*
Finland	*	*	–	2	20	13
Soviet	–	1	29	1	10	–
Poland	–	1	–	–	–	1
USA	–	7	–	7	–	6
Japan	–	4	14	1	10	1
Korea	–	1	–	–	–	1
N (firms)	2	161	7	170	10	344

Table 6.A3 includes countries that are listed as most important export market by at least 5 per cent of the firms in at least one of the regions in one of the countries. Figures do not add up to 100 due to rounding off decimals.

NOTE

1 Based on Havnes *et al.* (1994)

REFERENCES

Andersen, O. (1986) 'Regional Barriers to Exporting,' in K. Möller and M. Paltschick (eds) *Contemporary Research in Marketing*, Proceedings of the XVth Annual Conference of the European Marketing Academy, Vol 1, 287–96.

Andersen, O. (1991) 'Internasjonalisering i Mindre Bedrifter. Hva Betyr Bedriftens Beliggenhet?' i NordREFO 1991:1 Småforetaket-Økonomiens nye motor. Academic Press: Copenhagen.

Andersen, O. (1993) 'On the Internationalization Process of the Firm – A Critical Analysis', *Journal of International Business Studies*, 2: 209–31.

Blais, R.A., and Toulouse J.-M. (1990) 'National, Regional and World Patterns of Entrepreneurial Motivation?', *Journal of Small Business & Entrepreneurship*, 7, 2: 3–22.

Bonaccorsi, A. (1992) 'On the Relationship between Firms Size and Export Intensity', *Journal of International Business Studies*, Fourth Quarter, 605–35.

Cavusgil, S.T. (1984) 'Differences Among Exporting Firms Based on Their Degree of Internationalization', *Journal of Business Research*, 12: 195–208.

Chenery, H.B., Clark, P.G. and Cao-Pinna, V. (1953) 'The Structure and Growth of the Italian Economy', *US Mutual Security Agency*, Rome.

Culpan, R. (1989) 'Export Behavior of Firms: Relevance of Firm Size', *Journal of Business Research*, 18: 207–18.

Gripsrud, G. (1990) 'The Determinants for Export Decisions and Attitudes to a Distant Market: Norwegian Fishery Exports to Japan', *Journal of International Business Studies*, third quarter, 469–85.

Havnes, P.A., Sletten, J. and Saether, A. (1994) 'Is There a North–South Dimension to Internationalization of SMEs? An Exploratory Study of Firms in the Nordic Countries', paper presented at the *8th Nordic Conference on Small Business Research*, Halmstad University, 13–15 June, Halmstad.

Johanson, J., and Vahlne, J.-E. (1977) 'The Internationalization Process of the Firm – A Model of Knowledge Development and Increasing Foreign Market Commitment', *Journal of International Business Studies*, 8: 23–32.

Johanson, J. and Wiedersheim-Paul, F. (1975) 'The Internationalization of the Firm – Four Swedish Cases', *Journal of Management Studies*, 12, 3: 305–22.

Kanyak, E. and Ghauri, Pervez, N.G. (1987) 'Export Behavior of Small Swedish Firms', *Journal of Business Management*, 4: 26–32.

Manchini, C., and Prince, Y. (1993) 'Export Success of SMEs: An Empirical Study', *Research Report 9306/A, EIM/Manufacturing Industry*, Zoetermeer.

Nordkalottkomiteen (1977) *Handelsförbindelser på Nordkalotten*, Tromsø.

Nordkalottkomiteen (1990) *Handelsforbindelser på Nordkalotten*, Tromsø.

Schlegelmilch, B.B. and J.N. Crook, (1988) 'Firm-Level Determinants of Export Intensity', *Managerial and Decision Economics*, 9: 291–300.

Sriram, V. and Sapienza, H.J. (1991) 'An Empirical Investigation of the Role of Marketing for Small Exporters', *Journal of Small Business Management*, 29, 4: 33–43.

Welch, L.S. and Luostarinen, R.(1988) 'Internationalization: Evolution of a Concept', *Journal of General Management*, 14, 2: 34–64.

7   Export orientation

An econometric analysis

Yvonne Prince and Koos A. van Dijken

ABSTRACT

This chapter aims to contribute to the discussion on SMEs' exports by carrying out analyses on both the Dutch part of the Interstratos data set and the entire international data set. First, the discriminating factors between exporting and non-exporting firms are investigated. Second, the determinants of export ratios (export sales/total sales) are studied. The three most discriminating factors between exporting and non-exporting firms are: emphasis on competitive strategies, firm size and foreign language use. Although firm size is a discriminating factor between exporting and non-exporting firms, it appears, however, that when firms are exporting larger firms do not export a larger share of their sales. Factors like number of spoken languages, number of weeks stayed abroad, active search behaviour for export orders, and subsidiaries abroad affect export ratios positively.

INTRODUCTION

The internationalization of the Dutch economy is still increasing. This does not only affect firms which are active participants in the international market, but also firms which are primarily oriented to the home market. Due to the abolition of trade barriers within Europe and increasing technological progressiveness competition intensifies. In addition, the East European countries and the explosive growth of the Asian economies yield new opportunities and threats. At present, the developments in the international scene supersede what is called 'internationalization'. The new term to denote the present stage of internationalization is 'globalization'.[1]

In this chapter the emphasis is on factors explaining export performance. First, the discriminating factors between Dutch exporters and non-exporters are considered. Second, a model explaining the export ratio is presented. This study makes use of both the Dutch and the international 1991 data set, and preliminary analyses presented in Overveld (1993). It focuses on the main discriminating characteristics between Dutch exporting and non-exporting firms and sheds some light on the question: 'If firms do export a certain amount of their production, what factors influence the extent of exporting?'.

In other words, explanatory variables of the export ratio are considered. The final section offers a short summary of the empirical findings.

EXPORTERS VERSUS NON-EXPORTERS

In this section the Dutch data set is used. Data are available for 215 non-exporting and 175 exporting firms. Discriminant-analysis will reveal the discriminating characteristics between exporters and non-exporters. In other words, given the information gathered within the scope of the Interstratos-project, we will indicate some characteristics of the Dutch exporting firm.

Cavusgil and Nevin (1981) show that the determinants that explain whether firms are exporting or not can be classified in four groups: managements' export expectations, managements' commitment, differential firm advantages and managerial aspirations.

Ford and Leonidou (1991) present a review of the literature that considers internationalization as a process of increasing export involvement. Based on this strand of literature they argue that the export decision of firms is dependent on external as well as internal stimuli. The export decision is dependent on firm and management characteristics, as well as on characteristics of the firm's environment.[2] They also describe the stimuli and impediments to export success.[3] These factors can be classified into characteristics of the environment, firm and management, strategic variables and functional variables. The selection of the variables used in the present study are based on this classification. Functional factors, like existence and adequacy of export market plans and availability of sources to finance the export efforts, are not included due to lack of appropriate data measuring these characteristics.

Management characteristics

Since in SMEs the key exporting factor is the entrepreneur, some management characteristics are included in the analysis: the number of weeks spent in foreign countries during the last three years, the number of languages spoken by the management and the extent to which entrepreneurs are of the opinion that they should work to a business plan rather than by following their intuition.

Firm characteristics

The following firm characteristics are included in the analysis: number of employees, industrial sector, whether the firm is a subsidiary or not, the legal form of the firm, whether the firm is a subcontractor or not, and whether it is a private company or not.

Environment characteristics

As environmental variables the management's perception of market developments on the local as well as the national market are considered.

Strategic characteristics

Strategic aspects are measured by the extent of emphasis on several competitive strategies, the number of product groups, the number of customer groups, type of production (individual products, serial production or mass production), type of finished goods (for stock or by order) or whether the firm produces parts or semi-finished products.

Cavusgil and Naor (1987) also applied discriminant analysis to reveal differences between exporting and non-exporting firms. Their results show that exporters search more actively for information regarding international activities, exporters are active on the national market rather than on the local market, non-exporters are more of the opinion that exporting is a risky activity than exporters, the firm size of exporting firms is larger than that of non-exporting firms, knowledge of financing and planning is better developed in exporting than in non-exporting firms, and that exporters more often have the disposal of a national network. Management characteristics appear to have little influence in their analysis.

Dutch results

Discriminant analysis on the Dutch data set identifies which independent variables account for (most of) the differences between Dutch exporters and non-exporters. The results show that the three most discriminating factors between exporting and non-exporting firms are (in descending order): emphasis on competitive strategies; firm size (measured by the number of employees); and knowledge and use of

Table 7.1 The main discriminating characteristics between Dutch exporters and non-exporters, and their mean values

Discriminating factor	Non-exporting firms: mean values	Exporting firms: mean values
Emphasis on competitive strategies*	59.7	71.9
Firm size (in employees)	17.2	76.6
Number of spoken languages	2.5	3.6
Percentage of 'serial producers'	68.4	86.1
Percentage of 'stock producers'	20.2	48.7
Percentage of private firms	70.7	53.0

Note: * This variable is constructed by summing the scores 1 (less emphasis) up to 5 (strong emphasis) of 19 fields of competitive strategy. Hence, a score of 19 corresponds with less emphasis and 95 with strong emphasis on competition.

foreign languages. This latter result confirms the conclusion of Miesenbock (1988) where it is stated that 'the exporter is likely to speak more languages than the non-exporter'. Mugler and Miesenbock (1989) also found the number of foreign languages and firm size to discriminate significantly between non-exporters and exporters.

Table 7.1 shows the mean values of the factors that discriminate significantly between exporting and non-exporting firms for both groups of firms.[4] For example, on average the number of employees of a non-exporting firm is 17.2 employees while that of an exporting firm is considerably larger, i.e. 76.6 employees. To sum up, we may say that the profile of the Dutch exporting firm is a large firm, of which the management can express themselves in at least three languages and puts strong emphasis on competitive strategies, is not a private business and produces in series and for stock.

EXPLANATION OF EXPORT RATIOS

There is a huge literature on exporting of SMEs. See for example Miesenbock (1988) and Gemünden (1991) for extensive literature surveys. All studies agree that the barrier to start exporting is the most considerable hurdle that has to be taken in the process of internationalization. If firms have taken the crucial step of being involved in international business, such firms can then go through a few more stages of internationalization. In the literature several different approaches to classifying these stages to increasing internationalization can be found. For example, the gradual involvement process of Cavusgil (1984), the expansion strategies of Ansoff (1965), the generic competitive strategies of Porter (1980), the geographic segmentation strategies of Wind, Douglas and Perlmutter (1973)[5] and the entry stategies of Kotler (1980).[6]

Although there are numerous obstacles to going international (financial problems, lack of knowledge and information of foreign markets, cultural differences, language problems, technical specifications, transport costs, difficulties in distribution, lack of qualified staff, exchange rates, etc.) a large number of SMEs have made this risky step and are nowadays exporting some part of their production. In addition, van Elk (1992) shows that in the Netherlands the export volume of manufacturing SMEs (<100 employees) has been increasing to a larger extent than that of large firms (>100 employees) in the 1980s.

But what are the underlying factors for export performance? What characteristics lead to increasing export performance? In this section we will consider a model explaining export performance where export performance is expressed by the level of the export share (export sales as share of total sales). Also, the oft cited (positive) relation between firm size and export ratios will be tested.

Hypotheses

Below, hypotheses regarding the influences of the explanatory variables are postulated. Six variables correspond to the discriminating factors between exporting and non-exporting firms reported on pages 128–9 above. These factors are: emphasis on competitive factors; firm size; number of spoken languages; serial production; production of finished goods for stock[7]; and private company. By including them we test whether these factors also influence the extent of exporting.

Gemünden (1991) concluded in his overview of empirical studies on exporting that four factors are frequently found to affect export performance positively: firm size; export-oriented information activities; R&D-intensity; and export-oriented product adaptations and services. Therefore, apart from firm size, the use of education regarding international activities is also included. Data on R&D-intensity and the extent to which firms carry out export-oriented product adaptations are not available.

Furthermore, Miesenbock stated that 'the number of employees engaged in exporting, their educational background and the firm's personnel training are also variables associated with success' (Miesenbock 1988). The latter two aspects are captured by the variable use of education regarding international activities.

Foreign travel was also found to be a significant variable in favour of exporting. See Miesenbock (1988) for references. Therefore, the

Table 7.2 Hypothesized effects of variables explaining export share

Variable	Hypothesized effect
Emphasis on competitive strategies	positive
Firm size	positive
Number of spoken languages	positive
Serial production	positive
Production of finished goods for stock	positive
Private company	negative
Use of education regarding international activities	positive
Number of weeks stayed abroad	positive
Subsidiaries abroad	positive
Active search behaviour for foreign orders	positive
Percentage of foreign purchases	positive

number of weeks stayed abroad during the last three years is included to measure the effect of foreign travel. Also, some indicators of international involvement are included: subsidiaries abroad; active search behaviour for foreign orders; and the percentage of foreign purchases. It is expected that the higher the extent of international involvement the larger the amount of exports. See also Mugler and Miesenbock (1989). Table 7.2 lists the hypothesized effects of all independent variables included in the regression analysis.

Estimation results

Data from 816 European firms (in the participating countries) are used to test the hypotheses. The regression results are summarized in Table 7.3. Comparison of Tables 7.2 and 7.3 clearly shows that some

Table 7.3 Regression results; dependent variable: compared to export ratio

Variable	Coefficient	(T-value)
Intercept	−0.139	(−1.4)
Emphasis on competitive strategies	−0.002	(−1.5)
Firm size	−0.000	(0.4)
Number of spoken languages	0.040	(4.6)
Serial production	−0.047	(−2.3)
Production of finished goods	−0.087	(−4.7)
Private company	−0.031	(−1.6)
Use of education regarding int. activities	0.026	(1.4)
Number of weeks stayed abroad	0.003	(5.1)
Subsidiaries abroad	0.118	(5.9)
Active search behaviour for foreign orders	0.202	(9.3)
Percentage of foreign purchases	0.000	(0.8)

Note: Adjusted R^2: 0.27
Number of observations: 816

hypotheses are not confirmed by the empirical results. In addition, it is revealed that some of the six variables discriminating significantly between non-exporting and exporting firms do not explain the level of the export share. Moreover, only the coefficient of the number of spoken languages is statistically significant and has the expected sign. The more the firm's management is able to use foreign languages the higher the export share is. The coefficients of the variables emphasis on competitive strategies, firm size, and private company are not statistically significant.[8]

Prior to performing the regression all the explanatory variables were standardized to zero mean and unit variance so the estimated coefficients are not affected by the different scales of the explanatory variables.

The results on firm size correspond to those found by Mugler and Miesenbock (1989): firm size is a significant discriminator between exporters and non-exporters but has no significant influence on the export ratio. So our answer to the question 'Do larger firms also export a larger share of their sales?' is negative. Earlier empirical findings on firm size effects are mixed. Although some contradictory results can be attributed to the use of different measures of firm size, empirical studies measuring firm size by the number of employees, as is done in the present study, also yield ambiguous results. Cavusgil (1984) argues that

it may be more appropriate to view firm size as a concomitant variable rather than a causative factor...the true relationship it seems is not between size and export behaviour, but it is between various advantages which accrue from larger size, and export behaviour. In this sense, firm size serves as a proxy for various advantages associated with size.

(Cavusgil 1984)

Serial production and the production of finished goods for stock influence the export ratio negatively, while the earlier results have shown that there are more exporting than non-exporting firms which produce in series and for stock. At present we have no rational explanation for this; it seems to be a puzzling result. Maybe this disparity between empirical results can be attributed to the typical Dutch case.[9]

The number of weeks stayed abroad is more likely to lead to higher export performance than special training for export activities. Surprisingly, the use of education regarding international activities has no influence on export ratios. As expected, the extent of international commitment measured by the variables subsidiaries abroad[10] and active search behaviour for foreign orders, affects the degree of exporting positively. The percentage of foreign purchases which expresses to some extent the international involvement appears to have no effect on export ratios.

To sum up, the empirical results have revealed that:

- subsidiaries abroad correlate positively with the export ratio;
- the strategic variables serial production as type of production and producing finished goods for stock as type of finished goods affect the export ratio negatively; and
- management characteristics such as number of spoken languages, number of weeks stayed abroad and active search behaviour for foreign orders have a positive impact on export ratios.

SUMMARY

In this chapter we have investigated the discriminating factors between exporting and non-exporting firms in the Netherlands. Furthermore, an equation to explain the export ratio has been estimated. In our analyses we have made use of the Dutch part of the Interstratos data set as well as the entire international data set.

The empirical results have shown that the three most discriminating factors between exporting and non-exporting Dutch firms are: emphasis on competitive strategies; firm size, and foreign language use.

The export ratio is influenced by management characteristics such as number of spoken languages, number of weeks stayed abroad and active search behaviour for export orders, by whether products are produced in series, by whether finished products are made for stock, and by the presence of subsidiaries abroad.

Although firm size is a discriminating factor between exporting and non-exporting firms, it appears that among the exporting firms larger firms do not export a larger share of their sales than their smaller counterparts. This result is consistent with some earlier empirical investigations on the effects of firm size on export performance.

NOTES

1 See Humbert (1993) for a more extensive description of what is called 'globalization'.
2 See Ford and Leonidou (1991, Table 1.1) for a list of factors influencing the manager's attitude towards exporting.
3 See Ford and Leonidou (1991, Table 1.2) for a list of factors and obstacles to success in international trade.

4 Based on these six variables 80 per cent of the firms are correctly assigned to their respective groups.
5 See Putman (1993) for an application of the stages defined by Wind, Douglas and Perlmutter (1973): ethnocentrism, polycentrism and regiocentrism.
6 See Gankema, Zwart and Van Dijken (1993) for more details on the latter four international strategy classifications.
7 Miesenbock (1988), when reviewing a large literature on SMEs' exports concluded that the stock of finished goods was found to be a significant factor for success.
8 In this report the 5 per cent significance level is used.
9 The discriminant analysis revealing significant differences between exporting and non-exporting firms is based on Dutch firms only. A possible explanation is that the Dutch data set covers many subcontracters that are not highly specialized and produce much in series and for stock. These subcontracters do export but to a limited extent.
10 Of course, the direction of the causal relationship might be argued.

REFERENCES

Ansoff, H.I. (1965) *Corporate strategy*, New York: McGraw-Hill.
Cavusgil, S. Tamer (1984) 'Organizational characteristics associated with export activity', *Journal of Management Studies,* 21,1: 1–22.
Cavusgil, S. Tamer and Naor J. (1987) 'Firm and management characteristics as discriminators of export marketing activity, *Journal of Business Research,* 15: 221–35.
Cavusgil, S. Tamer and Nevin, J.R. (1981) 'Internal determinants of export marketing behaviour: an empirical investigation', *Journal of Marketing Research,* 18: 114–19.
Elk, J.W. van, (1992) 'SME export: scope, potential and beyond', paper presented at the conference *Entrepreneurship: Myths and Reality; Business Development Prospects and Policies,* Heraklion, Crete, Greece, September.
Ford, D. and Leonidou, L. (1991) 'Research developments in international marketing; a European perspective', in S.J. Paliwoda (ed.) *New perspectives on International Marketing,* London/New York: Routledge, 3–32.
Gankema, H.G.J., Zwart, P.S., and van Dijken, K.A. (1993) *Small Firms' International Strategies and Performance: a Comparison Between Dutch and Finnish Small Firms,* mimeo, Small Business Management: University of Groningen.
Gemünden, H.G. (1991) 'Success factors of export marketing: a meta-analytic critique of the empirical studies', in S.J. Paliwoda (ed.) *New Perspectives on International Marketing,* London/New York: Routledge, 33–63.
Haahti, A.J. (1993a) 'Interstratos-Internationalization of Strategic Orientations of European Small and Medium-Sized Enterprises', *EIASM Working Papers 1–93,* Brussels.
Haahti, A. (1993b) 'A cohort analysis of managers' experience, key success factors and export sales performance in small and medium European electronics firms in 1991 and 1992', *Interstratos Working Paper,* Brussels: November 4–6.

Humbert, M. (1993) 'Introduction: questions, constraints and challenges in the name of globalization', in M. Humbert (ed.) *The Impact of Globalization on Europe's Firms and Industries*, London: Pinter Publishers.

Kotler, P. (1980) *Marketing Management: Analysis, Planning and Control*, London: Prentice Hall.

Mancini, C. and Prince, Y.M. (1993) 'Export success of SMEs: an empirical study', *Research Report 9306/A*, EIM/Manufacturing Industry: Zoetermeer.

Miesenbock, K.J. (1988) 'Small business and exporting: a literature review', *International Small Business Journal*, 6, 2: 42–61.

Mugler, J. and Miesenbock, K.J. (1989) 'Determinants of increasing export involvement of small firms', paper presented at the *ICSB-Conference 1990*.

Overveld, I. van (1993) *Export Success of Small and Medium-sized Firms in Dutch Manufacturing*, (in Dutch Het exportsucces van het industriële midden- en kleinbedrijf: een Europese vergelijking), EIM/Manufacturing Industry: Zoetermeer.

Porter, M.E. (1980) *Competitive Strategy: Techniques for Analyzing Industries and Competitors*, New York: The Free Press.

Prince, Y.M. (1995) 'Export performance of SMEs', Research Report 9503/E, EIM, Zoetermeer.

Putman, G.A.J. (1993) *European Internationalization of Medium-sized Firms in Dutch Manufacturing* (in Dutch: Europese Internationalisering van de Middelgrote Ondernemingen in de Nederlandse Industrie), KPMG Klynveld Management Consultants.

Wind, Y., Douglas, S.P. and Perlmutter, H.V. (1973) 'Guidelines for developing international marketing strategies', *Journal of Marketing*, 37: 14–23.

8 Small firms' international strategies and performance

A comparison between Dutch and Finnish small firms

Harold G.J. Gankema, Peter S. Zwart and Koos A. van Dijken

INTRODUCTION

Due to the establishment of the Internal Market the international environment of small and medium-sized firms in Europe is changing rapidly. Since January 1993, the twelve EC countries form a common market in which nearly all physical, technical and fiscal trade barriers are faded away. The creation of the common market intensively influences the development of market conditions and competition today and in the near future. On the one hand, competition will get stronger because foreign competitors can now enter the domestic market without complex formalities. On the other hand this also goes for the domestic firms, which means that it is much easier to start export activities and to enter upon foreign markets. Uniformity in product requirements and less time consuming border controls will lower the cost of international trade.

In addition to these European developments, international trends in manufacturing industry such as globalization, acceleration of technical progress, shortening of product life cycles, changing relations between main and subcontractors and more international cooperation play a significant role. In this fierce international competition requirements concerning quality and logistics are increasing. Manufacturing industries – small as well as large – have to adapt to these trends to sustain this increasing international competition. To realize growth, flexibility and quality improvement both internationally and locally operating firms will have to broaden their view and reconsider their strategies based on the relative strengths and weaknesses of the firms and the international environment.

RESEARCH OBJECTIVES

A lot of research has been carried out concerning the motives of small firms for going international and the problems they face while exporting. Miesenböck (1988) distinguished between internal and external stimuli and found that the most important stimuli were external. Unsolicited orders from abroad, saturated home markets and more favourable market conditions are found to be important external stimuli (Bilkey and Tesar 1977; Rabino 1980; Kaynak and Stevenson 1982; Gankema and Zwart 1990). The most important internal stimuli are excessive capacity, a unique product, a differential advantage in technology or marketing and the attitude of the manager (Johnson and Czinkota 1982; Tesar and Tarleton 1982; Gankema and Zwart 1990).

Little attention, however, has been paid to the influence of international strategies on performance. Therefore, our research does not examine the motives of small firms and the problems they met, but concentrates on the international strategies Dutch and Finnish small firms implemented and the influence of these strategies on performance.

Our research objectives are to determine:

1 which strategies are implemented at various levels by Dutch and Finnish small firms;
2 which strategies seem to be most successful;
3 which combinations of strategies from various levels are found most frequently;
4 which of these combinations of strategies are found to be most successful; and
5 whether differences exist between both countries concerning the above questions.

THEORETICAL BACKGROUND

In the literature the concept of strategy is not unequivocal, because various classifications are made. The most well-known classifications are the expansion strategies of Ansoff (1965), the generic competitive strategies of Porter (1980), and from an international point of view the geographic segmentation strategies of Wind, Douglas and Perlmutter (1973) and Kotler's entry strategies (1988).

Ansoff (1965) classified four potential strategies at the corporate level, namely: market penetration; market development; product development; and diversification. This classification of these 'corporate strategies' is based on two criteria: (1) whether or not the future products are new to the organization; and (2) whether or not the future markets are new to the organization. Decisions concerning entering new markets and choices concerning which products will be introduced in these markets have long-term consequences for running the firm (Leeflang 1987). Kotler (1980) argues that management should first review whether there are any further opportunities for improving the performance of its existing business. Ansoff has proposed a product/market expansion grid for detecting new intensive growth opportunities.

- Choosing a market penetration strategy the firm tries to gain more market share with current products on current markets by encouraging current customers to use more, making competitors' customers switch brand or convincing non-users to buy the product. One can expect a great number of small firms acting like this.
- Selecting a market development strategy the firm is looking for new markets (other segments or abroad) the needs of which are met by current products. Seifert and Ford (1989) and Gronhaug and Kvitastein (1992) found that small firms often use current products starting export activities.
- A product development strategy is used when the former strategies offer insufficient opportunities and one has to consider product development possibilities.
- A diversification strategy means introducing new products to new customers. This makes sense only when good opportunities can be found outside the present business (Kotler 1980). Porter (1990) indicated that European firms should learn from the American firms in the 1980s and concentrate on their core business.

Porter (1980) concentrates on the competitive advantage of the firm. He stated that a firm has to choose very clearly from one of the three generic competitive strategies he classified: cost leadership; focus; or differentiation. These strategies concern the position of the firms among their competitors.

- Overall cost leadership means that the firm can produce and distribute at lower costs than competitors, e.g. because of economies of scale.
- A strategy of differentiation means that the firm is exploiting a competitive differential advantage in e.g. quality, design, service or brand. The product clearly distinguishes itself from other products.
- In choosing a focus strategy a firm is concentrating on one or more narrow market segments and keeps looking for new niches to serve.

Porter (1980) claims that firms who do not make an explicit choice, cannot be well positioned. Porter describes this situation as 'stuck in the middle'. Dess and Davis (1984) found that these firms performed significantly worse and they concluded that a firm cannot successfully implement various generic competition strategies at the same time. Miller and Friesen (1986) confirmed these results, but also indicated that big firms producing durables sometimes succeeded in being cost leader and at the same time successfully pursued a strategy of differentiation. Aaker (1993), on the other hand, distinguishes two basic strategies, cost leadership and differentiation, and argues that a focus strategy can very well be combined with one of these strategies.

A number of factors like leadership style, managers' attitudes towards foreign trade, history, culture, etc. account for the strategic predisposition of a firm on the international market. Wind, Douglas and Perlmutter (1973) defined four strategic predispositions that determine how a manager participates and segments the international market: ethnocentrism, polycentrism, regiocentrism and geocentrism.

- Ethnocentrism is the predisposition in which all strategic decisions are guided by the conditions of the domestic market. Orders from abroad are neglected or treated as domestic. Products are not adapted.
- Polycentrism is a predisposition in which strategic decisions are tailored to meet the various market conditions in every country in which the firm competes. Products and marketing policy are adapted to every country to which the firm is exporting.
- Regiocentrism and Geocentrism are predispositions in which strategic decisions are based on market conditions which several countries (a region) or global segments have in common. Products are standardized as much as possible. In this study these two are taken together as a global orientation.

The (implicit) choice of one of these geographic segmentation strategies has enormous consequences for the international marketing policy. The benefits of adaptation have to be weighed against those of standardization.

Once a firm has decided to fulfil an occasional order from abroad or to introduce a product to a foreign market, it has to determine the best mode of distribution or market entry. This broad scale of entry strategy with increasing amount of commitment, risk and potential profit include: indirect exporting; direct exporting; licensing; joint ventures; and direct investment (Kotler 1980).

- An indirect export strategy means that the firm works through domestic-based independent middlemen. Goods are produced in the home country.
- When choosing a direct export strategy, the firm handles its own export. Goods are still produced in the home country, but they are

sold by a domestic-based export department, export sales representatives, or foreign-based agents or subsidiaries.

● Licensing represents an agreement with a foreign licensee, offering
the right to use a manufacturing process, trade mark, patent, etc.
for a fee or royalty. This study does not include this entry strategy.

● In joint ventures the firm joins with foreign investors to create a
local business in which they share joint ownership and control.

● A direct investment includes an investment in foreign-based assembly or manufacturing facilities.

The choice of entry strategy is strongly related to the differences
and similarities concerning culture (Kogut and Singh 1988) and market structure (Erramilli 1991) between domestic and foreign market.
This implies that an exporting firm can choose various entry strategies
at the same time, depending on the country it is exporting to. Ethnocentric firms of course, may also decide not to sell abroad.

A hierarchy of strategies

The four classifications described above have little in common and are
unrelated to each other. A distinction between primary and secondary
strategies was made by Piest (1990). Primary strategic options are
options concerning the product/market combinations being served. A
clear example of these options is the classifications of Ansoff (1965).
Secondary strategic options include the position in the environment
circumscribed by the primary strategic option chosen. Porter's generic
competitive strategies (1980) clearly are included in this category.

This model now can be extended in an international context. Taking
the corporate strategy and the positioning on the domestic market as a
starting point, the next step in the internationalization of the firm will
be guided by the attitude, cultural and historical background of the
manager. His predisposition determines how the foreign market is
perceived and segmented. Product adaptation and standardization
must be weighed against each other and finally the mode of market
entry must be decided upon.

Theoretically a firm should, in the international strategic decision-
making process, go through a hierarchy of strategies at various levels
and make at each level a deliberate choice consistent with choices at
the higher levels and the strengths and weaknesses of the firm. Using
the classifications of Ansoff (1965), Porter (1980), Wind, Douglas and
Perlmutter (1973) and Kotler (1980) we suggest the hierarchy of
strategies shown in Figure 8.1 as a starting point.

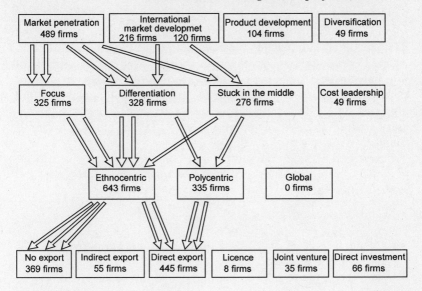

Figure 8.1 Hierarchy of strategies

RESEARCH DESIGN

Data

The data used was generated by the Interstratos group in 1991. It was derived in this study from 978 Dutch firms and 299 Finnish (see also Haahti *et al.* 1993).

Method of analysis

Cluster analysis procedures were utilized to determine which strategies firms chose at each level, according to the procedure recommended by Punj and Stewart (1983). This procedure is as follows:

1 Apply Ward's hierarchical clustering method.
2 Obtain a preliminary cluster solution.
3 Select number of clusters.
4 Perform iterative partitioning.
5 Final solution.

In step 1 the distance between two clusters is calculated as the sum of squares between the two clusters summed over all variables (Ward's method). According to Punj and Stewart (1983) this generally generates the best solution. As a result of this method a preliminary cluster solution is found in step 2. In step 3 the number of clusters is selected based on three criteria: (a) the relative size of the clustering coefficients; (b) the variance between the clusters; and (c) the number of respondents belonging to a cluster. Outliers are removed and the centroids of the clusters are obtained. In step 4 an iterative partitioning procedure is performed, using the cluster centroids of the preliminary analysis as a starting point. In step 5 the final cluster solution is found.

In order to partition the sample into homogeneous groups of firms with the same strategies at each level, the following variables are used in the cluster analysis:

- Market expansion strategies:
  - the number of types of product
  - the percentage of sales of the three most important products
  - the number of types of customer
  - the percentage of sales to the three most important customers
  - the export/total sales ratio
  - the local sales/total sales ratio
- Generic competition strategies:
  A set of 19 variables is used. This set of variables concerned questions about the most important factors in achieving success and were measured on a 5-point scale from no importance to very high importance. To find out whether these 19 variables have some underlying dimensions in common, a factor analysis was first carried out. This resulted in the following six factors used as input in the cluster analysis:
  1 Marketing (after sales service, creativity, sales force, design)
  2 Management (quality of management, reputation, public relations)
  3 Costs (lowest prices, lowest costs)
  4 Technology (up-to-date technology, solve technological problems)
  5 Flexibility (respond quickly to changes, modify products)
  6 Product quality
- Geographic segmentation strategies:
  - hunting for orders from abroad
  - how often orders were received from abroad
  - ability to modify products.
- Market entry strategies
  - agents in the Netherlands

- Dutch manufacturers who eventually export
- Dutch distributors who export
- agents abroad
- direct to customers abroad
- licences
- distribution subsidiaries abroad
- manufacturing subsidiaries abroad

In order to determine the success of the various strategies and to describe the firms implementing a certain strategy the following variables are used as background variables in the cluster analysis:

- type of industry
- number of employees
- sales
- export sales
- export sales ratio
- sales per employee

RESULTS OF THE RESEARCH

Results in The Netherlands

The overall results of the cluster analyses are shown at Figure 8.2.

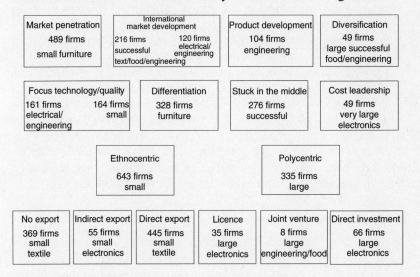

Figure 8.2 Strategies implemented by Dutch small firms

Market expansion strategies

From the results shown in Figure 8.2 we can see that most Dutch firms have implemented a market penetration strategy. These firms hardly sell abroad and concentrate on sales in the local area. They are the smaller ones and their sales turnover per employee is the lowest of all.

The firms with a market development strategy can be divided into those with a national and those with an international orientation. National market developers are not hunting for orders from abroad, but are responding to incidental foreign orders. They are quite successful.

International market developers are hunting for orders from abroad as well as responding to incidental orders. Their export sales ratio is high.

Most of the firms who have chosen a product development strategy are quite successful.

Diversifying firms hunt for orders from abroad as well as responding to incidental orders. They are the larger firms and they are the most successful ones in terms of sales and export sales per employee. Both the sectors electronic and mechanical engineering are strongly internationally oriented. The other sectors on average concentrate on market penetration.

Generic competitive strategies

Most of the Dutch firms are trying to differentiate themselves from others by stressing marketing, technology and product quality. Only a few of the larger firms are concentrating on cost leadership. They are very much internationally oriented and quite successful.

Firms focusing on technology (innovation) are far more internationally oriented then those that are focusing on doing the best job possible (quality). Remarkably, both these types of strategy are less successful than all the others. Even the large group of firms that are not able to set any priorities is more successful.

Mechanical engineering firms focus on technology more than the average, while electronic engineering firms pursue cost leadership. Textile and clothing firms focus on quality more than average.

Geographic segmentation strategies

None of the Dutch firms has a global point of view. On the contrary, most of the small firms can be characterized as ethnocentric. The polycentric firms however, are larger, more successful and more internationally oriented.

Market entry strategies

A large group of the Dutch small firms does not export at all. The most popular entry strategy among exporters is direct exporting, followed by indirect exporting. The larger firms are using direct investment, licence and joint venture as an entry strategy as well.

Paths through the hierarchy of strategies

To get any insight into the relationship between the strategies chosen at each level, all the possible paths through the hierarchy of strategies were specified. Nine of these paths are followed by 20 or more firms. Paths with frequencies lower than 20 firms are not shown (see Figure 8.3).

Remarkably, the four paths with a focus strategy on the second level are not successful. Also unsuccessful is the combination of differentiation with no export. The most successful combinations of strategies in order of decreasing success are:

- international market development/stuck in the middle/polycentric/ direct export
- international market development/differentiation/polycentric/direct export
- market penetration/stuck in the middle/ethnocentric/no export

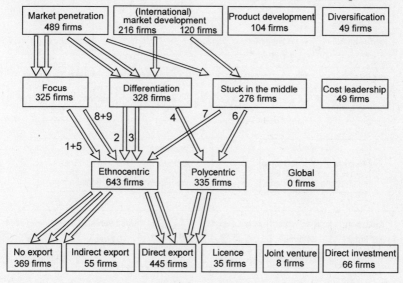

Figure 8.3 The most frequent paths to exporting in the Netherlands

- market penetration/differentiation/ethnocentric/direct export

Although less frequent the following paths were also found to be very successful:

- product development/stuck in the middle/polycentric/direct export
- diversification/cost leadership/polycentric/direct export

Results in Finland

The overall results of the cluster analyses are shown at Figure 8.4.

Market expansion strategies

From the results shown in Figure 8.4 we can see that most Finnish firms have followed a market penetration strategy. These firms are the very small ones and their sales turnover per employee is the lowest of all. The degree of internationalization is low.

The firms with an international market development strategy can be characterized as the larger successful ones, internationally oriented, and hunting for orders from abroad. They lay much emphasis on technology. Most of the firms that have chosen a product development strategy are medium-sized. The export sales ratio is quite low, although many of these firms indicated they had just started exporting.

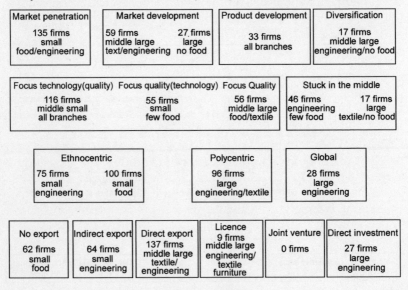

Figure 8.4 Strategies implemented by Finnish small firms

Diversifying firms are medium sized and lay strong emphasis on marketing. They export more than average and have a high sales volume per employee. Both the sectors textile and mechanical engineering are strongly internationally oriented. The food industry especially concentrates on market penetration.

Generic competitive strategies

Most of the Finnish firms are implementing a focus strategy. This large group can be divided into a smaller group that concentrates on both quality and technology and a group that primarily concentrates on quality alone. The other firms have very clearly not chosen one of Porter's options and are therefore actually stuck in the middle. These firms are the larger ones and are more internationally oriented. The food industry is mainly focusing on quality, while mechanical engineering is also focusing on technology or they may be described as internationally oriented and stuck in the middle.

Geographic segmentation strategies

A small group of Finnish firms has a global point of view. They are highly involved in exporting and are hunting for orders from abroad. Products are not adapted. Most of the firms however, are ethnocentric and sell to none or only a few countries. They are the smaller ones with low sales volumes and export sales ratios.

Polycentric firms are concentrating on adapting products. They emphasize marketing and are hunting for orders from abroad. The food industry has mainly an ethnocentric point of view, while the textile and mechanical engineering industries have a more international attitude.

Market entry strategies

Most of the Finnish firms are involved in exporting. Most popular is direct exporting. Remarkably joint venturing was not mentioned once. Most of the non-exporters are small firms of the food industry. Most involved in international activities are firms in the mechanical engineering industry.

Paths through the hierarchy of strategies

To get insight into the relationship between the strategies chosen at each level, all the possible paths through the hierarchy of strategies were

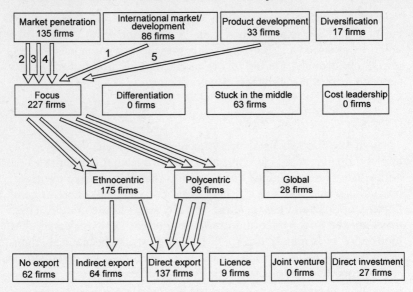

Figure 8.5 The most frequent paths to exporting in Finland

specified. Five of these paths are followed by six firms or more. Paths with frequencies lower than six firms are not shown (see Figure 8.5).

Very remarkably, the four most frequent combinations of strategies are not successful. The only successful path in Finland seems to be path number 5:

● product development/focus/polycentric/direct export

This path is implemented by firms from all industries, but these firms clearly are the larger ones.

The most successful combinations of strategies in both countries

The most frequent combinations of strategies are definitely not the most successful. In the Netherlands, also, two less frequent paths not mentioned in Figure 8.3 were found to be very successful. The most successful paths in both countries are shown in Figure 8.6.

Very remarkably a focus strategy is only successful in Finland in combination with product development, a polycentric strategic orientation and direct exporting. Most striking, and in contradiction to Porter's theory, are the very successful combinations implemented by the Dutch firms, with no outspoken strategic choice at the second level.

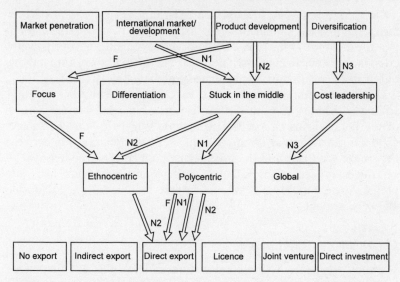

Figure 8.6 The most successful paths to exporting in the Netherlands and Finland

CONCLUSION

Strategies

The results summarized in Figures 8.2 and 8.4 show on the one hand great similarity, but on the other hand remarkable differences between Dutch and Finnish small firms.

Concerning Ansoff's expansion strategies, the resemblance is striking. In both countries half of the firms are implementing a strategy of penetration; a third have been working on market development, about one out of ten is concentrating on product development and a very small group diversify.

Great differences exist on the level of Porter's competitive strategies. In the Netherlands all strategic options suggested by Porter are found, differentiation being most popular, followed by a remarkably successful 'stuck in the middle' small group concentrating on cost leadership. The rest of the firms focus on either technology or quality. Neither of the focus strategies are successful. In Finland on the contrary, a focus strategy is very popular, but only in combination with other successful strategies. No cost leadership or differentiation strategy was found. As in the Netherlands, about a quarter of the Finnish firms is just stuck in the middle.

On the level of Wind, Douglas and Perlmutter's segmentation strategies, again great similarities exist between the two countries. About two thirds of the firms have an ethnocentric orientation. In the Netherlands the other firms have a polycentric strategy but in Finland one out of ten seems to have implemented a global (standardized) strategy.

Only some minor differences exist on the fourth level of entry strategies. Almost all Finnish firms export while a substantial portion of the Dutch firms choose not to export. When firms export, direct export is most popular in both countries. Also a relationship between the size of the firms and the involvement and risk in accompanying a certain entry strategy is found in both countries. Larger firms are prepared to be more involved and to take more risks when choosing an entry strategy.

Combinations of strategies

The most frequently found combinations of strategies, as summarized in Figures 8.3 and 8.5 show some remarkable differences. Quite clearly, the Dutch firms are in general less internationally oriented than the Finnish firms. In the Netherlands the combination of market penetration/focus/ethnocentric/no export is found most often while in Finland the combination International market development/focus/ polycentric/direct export is the most frequent one. None of these popular combinations is very successful though.

A remarkable difference between the two countries is that even ethnocentric Finnish firms are almost all involved in exporting (in)directly, while most ethnocentric Dutch firms are not exporting at all. It clearly shows that in both countries the most frequently found paths are not the most successful ones.

The results clearly show differences in international strategic behaviours and the success of various combinations of strategies between Finland and the Netherlands. Almost all Finnish firms are internationally involved. Even when they are ethnocentric, they are still capable of handling export activities. Finnish firms therefore should concentrate on product development for foreign markets and export directly.

A substantial proportion of the Dutch firms concentrate on the domestic market. Until now this is not unsuccessful. More successful however is international market development, implementing a polycentric segmentation strategy and exporting directly. For the larger Dutch firms product development or diversification can be profitable, if they do not stick to an ethnocentric point of view.

Acknowledgement

The authors thank Walraad van Dalen for his contribution and assistance in the preparation of this paper.

REFERENCES

Aaker, D.A. (1993) *Marktgericht Strategisch Beleid*, Academic Service, Schoonhoven, (Dutch translation: Developing Business Strategies – 3rd edn).

Ansoff, H.I. (1965) *Corporate Strategy*, New York: McGraw-Hill.

Bilkey, W.J. and Tesar, G.(1977) 'The Export Behavior of Smaller Sized Wisconsin Manufacturing Firms', *Journal of International Business Studies*, Spring-Summer, 93–8.

Dess, G.G. and Davis, P.S. (1984) 'Porter's Generic Strategies as Determinants of Group Membership and Organizational Performance', *Academy of Management Journal*, 27.3: 467–88.

Erramilli, M. (1991) 'The Experience Factor in Foreign Market Entry Behavior of Service Firms', *Journal of International Business Studies*, third quarter.

Gankema, H.G.J. and Zwart, P.S. (1990) *Het Exportgedrag van het Midden-en Kleinbedrijf in Noord-Nederland,* Memorandum van het Instituut voor Economisch Onderzoek, Faculteit der Economische Wetenschappen Rijksuniversiteit Groningen, no. 393.

Grönhaug, K. and Kvitastein, O. (1992) 'Expansion Strategies in International Markets: An Exploratory Study', *Scandinavian International Business Review*, 1,1: 57–70.

Haahti, A.J. *et al.* (1993) 'Internationalization of Strategic Orientations of European Small and Medium Enterprises', Interstratos, *EIASM Working Papers 1–93*, Brussels.

Johnson, W.J. and Czinkota, M.R. (1982) 'Managerial Motivations as Determinants of Industrial Export Behaviour', in M.R. Czinkota and G. Tesar (eds) *Export Management: An international context*, New York: Praeger, pp. 3–18.

Kaynak, E. and Stevenson, L.(1982) 'Export Orientation of Nova Scotia Manufacturers', in M.R. Czinkota and G.Tesar (eds) *Export Management: An International Context*, New York: Praeger, pp. 132–149.

Kogut, B. and Singh, H. (1988) 'The Effect of National Culture on the Choice of Entry Mode', *Journal of International Business Studies*, Fall.

Kotler, P. (1980) *Marketing Management, Analysis, Planning and Control*, Englewood Cliffs, N.J.: Prentice Hall, Inc.

Leeflang, P.S.H. (1987) *Probleemgebied Marketing, een Management Benadering*, 2e druk, Leiden-Antwerpen: H.E. Stenfert Kroese B.V.

Miesenböck, K.J. (1988) 'Small Business and Exporting: A Literature Review', *International Small Business Journal*, 6.2: 42–61.

Miller, D. and Friesen, P.H. (1986) 'Porter's Generic Strategies and Performances: an Empirical Examination with American Data', *Organization Studies*, 7.1: 37–55.

Piëst, E. (1990) *Zoeken, Wegen en Kiezen*, Groningen:Wolters-Noordhoff.

Porter, M.E. (1980) *Competitive Strategy*, New York: The Free Press.

Porter, M.E. (1990) 'De Doodlopende Weg naar Europa 1992', *The Economist*, NRC Handelsblad, 4 juli 1990, supplement ECONOMIE, pp. 4–5.

Punj, G and Stewart, D.W. (1983) 'Cluster Analysis in Marketing Research: Review and Suggestions for Application', *Journal of Marketing Research*, May: 134–48.

Rabino, S.(1980) 'An Examination of Barriers to Exporting Encountered by Small Manufacturing Companies', *Management International Review*, 20.1: 67–73.

Seifert, B. and Ford, J. (1989) 'Are Exporting Firms Modifying Their Product, Pricing and Promotion Policies?', *International Marketing Review*, 6.6: 53–67.

Tesar, G. and Tarleton, J.S. (1982) 'Comparison of Wisconsin and Virginia Small- and Medium-sized Exporters: Aggressive and Passive Exporters', in M.R. Czinkota and G.Tesar (eds) *Export Management: An International Context*, New York: Praeger, pp. 85–113.

Wind, Y., Douglas, S.P. and Perlmutter, H.V. (1973) 'Guidelines for Developing International Marketing Strategies', *Journal of Marketing*, 37: 14–23.

9 Internationalization and ownership

Family versus non-family enterprises

Rik Donckels and Ria Aerts

INTRODUCTION

Internationalization is a continous process happening all over the world. The participation of Small and Medium Enterprises (SMEs) in the internationalization process is increasing (European Network for SME Research (1993)). There are several reasons for this growing interest. We will classify them into two categories: macroeconomic and microeconomic reasons.

Ali and Swiercz (1991) view the international competitiveness of America's small and medium-sized businesses as playing a crucial role in the future competitiveness of the United States. They highlighted the importance of SMEs which are actively involved in international trade in highly competitive countries such as Germany and Japan. In these countries, SMEs realize a large proportion of exports. Edmunds and Khoury (1986) believe that increasing the exports of small firms can generate 'lasting broad benefits' not only for small firms but for the economy as a whole. Hanvey (1993) demonstrated that exporting SMEs created far more jobs than non-exporting firms. Between 1989 and 1992 employment rose in his sample of exporting firms in Northern Ireland by 7 per cent compared with 1 per cent in the non-exporting firms. So the macroeconomic significance of the internationalization of SMEs is chiefly expressed in the creation of employment and the improvement of regional competitiveness.

At the microeconomic level, several advantages can be cited (Ferguson and Gibb 1993):

- companies may become more competitive through cheaper sourcing or subcontracting across national boundaries;
- companies will be able to prepare for threats and take advantage of opportunities if they have an effective international environment scanning process;

- companies may be able to achieve economies of scale through market development;
- companies may be able to find overseas markets which offer higher profit margins;
- companies operating in niche markets may find servicing similar niches in other countries less of a risk than diversifying into additional niches in the home market;
- it may be possible to extend the product life cycle through overseas market development; and
- companies may be able to establish strategic alliances to maintain the critical mass required for research and development.

So there appear to be sufficient motives for SMEs to go international.

In this article a comparison is made between family businesses (FBs) and non-family businesses (NFBs) small and medium-sized enterprises with respect to the internationalization phenomenon. Why family versus non-family businesses? We can cite two important reasons for this. First, various studies show that the majority of SMEs in different countries are family businesses (Welsch 1991; Donckels and Hoebeke 1992; Neubauer 1992; Donckels and Aerts 1993). In the Stratos survey (1990), some 1,132 SMEs from eight countries were examined to see whether they were family businesses or not. The percentages varied from nearly 52 per cent to more than 83 per cent. Second, several studies have already indicated specific and significant differences between non-family businesses and family businesses (Donckels and Fröhlich 1991; Gallo and Luostarinen 1991; Donckels and Aerts 1993). For instance, family businesses are more opposed to change. They are characterized by conservatism and an aversion to risk. The internationalization process represents a process of change: changes towards new products, operations and markets, with distinct customers and competitors; changes in the information systems, planning systems, controlling systems and in the organizational structure, with new people and responsibilities; and changes in the management attitudes, philosophies, etc. (Gallo and Luostarinen 1991). Family businesses therefore tend to be found more in the category of less internationally active firms (Aerts 1992).

QUESTIONS

Two research questions need to be answered.

Family versus non-family enterprises: intensity of internationalization

The literature survey has shown that family SMEs are less internationally active than non-family SMEs. In the first part of this paper we ask ourselves whether this also applies to the different forms of international activity. We will examine more particularly whether, compared with non-family SMEs, family SMEs are less inclined to:

- import;
- export;
- realize their turnover through export;
- have branches abroad;
- have production plants abroad;
- take licences from foreign companies;
- give licences to foreign companies; and
- enter into a joint venture with a foreign company.

Internationally active family versus non-family enterprises: strategies

If the first part of this paper reveals that family businesses are less internationally active than non-family businesses, we will progress further to examine which factors play a role in internationally active NFBs to maintain or strengthen their competitive position, and which play a smaller or no role. This outline of important factors can show family businesses the way to more successful international achievements.

METHODOLOGY

This paper is based on responses to the survey which formed part of the Interstratos project (Haahti 1993). We use the database of the first year of investigation (1991) with data from the following countries: Austria, Belgium, the Netherlands, Switzerland, UK, Norway, Sweden and Finland. Table 9.1 gives an overview of the data per sector and company size. From the questionnaire we selected the questions relating to internationalization (import, export, share of export in total turnover excluding VAT, branch, production unit, giving licences, taking licences, and joint venture). These questions, except those concerning export share in turnover, were answered yes or no. Then the entrepreneurs in the sample rated 19 success factors (Appendix) according to a five-point scale (no importance, low importance, medium importance, high importance and very high importance). The five classes were reduced to two classes, since we are only interested in the firms that attach on the one hand no, little or medium importance and on the other hand relatively great importance to the factor. The

Table 9.1 Interstratos sample by size class and sector (first survey, 1991) (absolute and relative frequencies)

Size class (numer of employees)	Textiles/ clothing		Electronics		Sector food		Furniture making		Mechanical engineering		Total	
	N	%	N	%	N	%	N	%	N	%	N	%
00–09	419	8	198	4	308	6	336	7	344	7	1605	32
10–19	160	3	135	3	191	4	233	5	246	5	965	19
20–49	211	4	185	4	169	3	230	5	299	6	1094	22
50–99	110	2	106	2	115	2	126	3	214	4	671	14
100–499	101	2	123	3	131	3	86	2	203	4	644	13
Total	1001	20	747	15	914	18	1011	20	1306	26	4979	100

success factors were selected on the basis of relevant literature (Bamberger 1986; Stratos 1990). The yes/no question on family businesses was naturally also included. A family business is defined as a company where at least 50 per cent of the capital is held by one family.

In order to answer the first question, we will use the chi-square test. As the significance level, we used an alpha value of 0.05. In Table 9.2, we indicated the p-values as calculated by the Statistical Analyses System (SAS) program.

Table 9.2 χ^2 analysis of internationalization by family and non-family businesses

		FB	NFB	Probability
Import (N = 4119)	Yes	69	80	0.000
	No	31	20	
Export (N = 4102)	Yes	22	27	0.002
	No	78	73	
Export/total sales (N = 4967)	<= 50	93	85	0.000
	> 50	7	15	
Export/total sales (N = 4967)	<= 25	87	77	0.000
	> 25	13	23	
Branch abroad (N = 4435)	Yes	13	23	0.000
	No	87	77	
Production plant abroad (N = 4435)	Yes	8	12	0.000
	No	92	88	
Taking licences (N = 4449)	Yes	8	16	0.000
	No	92	84	
Giving licences (N = 4413)	Yes	6	10	0.000
	No	94	90	
Joint venture (N = 4967)	Yes	3	6	0.000
	No	97	94	

The second part of the paper is based on the use of logit regression analysis (Appendix).

RESULTS

Are family businesses less internationally active?

The chi-square analysis gives the following conclusions:

- Fewer FB than NFB import
- Fewer FB than NFB export
- Fewer FB than NFB derive more than 25 per cent of their turnover from export
- Fewer FB than NFB derive more than 50 per cent of their turnover from export
- Fewer FB than NFB take licences from foreign companies
- Fewer FB than NFB give licences to foreign companies
- Fewer FB than NFB have a branch abroad
- Fewer FB than NFB have a production plant abroad
- Fewer FB than NFB enter into a joint venture with a foreign firm

So the question 'Are family businesses less internationally active?' can be answered affirmatively. In every form of internationalization we find more family businesses in the non-active category. Also when we consider export intensity, we see that family businesses again come second to non-family businesses.

Importance of various factors per internationalization form

Importing

There is only one factor to which FB attach more importance than NFB, namely reputation and local image. On the other hand, there are ten factors to which NFBs attach more importance than FB. NFB primarily emphasize the quality of management, as well as the distribution and sales staff. Market share and low cost levels are also given the necessary attention. Furthermore, NFBs aim at innovative and customer-oriented products, since ability to modify products, technology, ability to solve technical problems, product design and brand image, after-sales service and creativity score better among NFB than among FB. Consequently, NFB attach more importance to product, price and promotion than do FB. Table 9.3 summarizes these findings.

Table 9.3 Factors for importing

Compared with NFBs, FBs attach more importance to	Compared with NFBs, FBs attach less importance to
Reputation and local image	Quality of management
	Distribution and selling staff
	Market share
	Low cost level
	Ability to modify products
	Technology
	Ability to solve technical problems
	Product design and brand image
	Creativity

Exporting

Reputation, local image and personal contacts, as well as customer relations, are given more emphasis by FB than by NFB. The latter, though, attach more importance to quality of management, technology and the ability to solve technical problems. FB appear to prefer close contacts with their customers. This, however, becomes more difficult when the customer is based abroad. NFB try to strengthen their position on these foreign markets by offering high-tech products through competent managers. This means that they concentrate more on creating a good quality product, which can result in a good reputation. Table 9.4 summarizes these findings.

Table 9.4 Factors for exporting

Compared with NFBs, FBs attach more importance to	Compared with NFBs, FBs attach less importance to
Reputation and local image	Quality of management
Customer relations	Technology
	Ability to solve technical problems

Branch abroad

No factor is considered more important by FB than by NFB. NFB, on the other hand, concern themselves to a large extent with distribution and sales staff. The following factors, too, are rated more highly by NFB than by FB: ability to solve technical problems, pricing policy, product design and brand image, ability to modify products, technology, financial strength and creativity. These findings are summarized in Table 9.5.

Table 9.5 Factors for branch abroad

Compared with NFBs', *FBs attach more importance to*	*Compared with NFBs,* *FBs attach less importance to*
No factors	Distribution and selling staff
	Ability to solve technical problems
	Pricing policy
	Product design and brand image
	Ability to modify products
	Technology
	Financial strength
	Creativity

Production plant abroad

FB find creativity more important than do NFB. Distribution and sales staff, though, are considered more important by NFB than by FB. These findings are summarized in Table 9.6.

Table 9.6 Factors for production plant abroad

Compared with NFBs, *FBs attach more importance to*	*Compared with NFBs,* *FBs attach less importance to*
Creativity	Distribution and selling staff

Taking licences from foreign companies

No factor is rated more highly by FB than by NFB. The same goes for NFB versus FB.

Giving licences to foreign companies

Here, too, no significant differences per factor are observed.

Joint venture

No difference between FB and NFB is found.

CONCLUSION

Fewer FB feature as players on the international scene. Non-family businesses are the ones that call the tune when it comes to import, export, branch and/or production plant abroad, taking licences from and giving licences to foreign companies, as well as the setting up of joint ventures with foreign companies.

Since internationalization yields macroeconomic as well as micro-economic benefits, it seems a good idea to set up supporting actions which will increase the chances of international success for family businesses. In this article we tried to discover to which factors the internationally active non-family businesses attach more importance than the internationally active family businesses. With respect to import, export, branch and/or production plant abroad, NFB under-line the importance of high-quality staff and management. In the first three forms, the innovation aspect is also clearly given far more attention by NFB than by FB. The FB, on the other hand, are significantly more concerned with their reputation in import and export. These conclusions bear out the fact that FB tend to have a more local culture which drives them to operate the business locally and employ managers without international experience. The FB are accustomed to having a functional, hierarchical responsibility struc-ture with managers who are not very integrative and 'resist' the incorporation of international activities due to the novelty it involves (Gallo and Sveen 1991).

Nevertheless, the family nature of FBs provide these firms with indisputable assets: knowledge and experience, dedication and swift-ness of decision. Yet the family nature of FB is an obstacle to expan-sion rather than a stimulus for growth (Donckels 1993). That is why for these firms a professional management and a greater appreciation of innovations would constitute a good preparation for the interna-tional arena.

SUGGESTIONS FOR FURTHER RESEARCH

The world of family and non-family SMEs is a highly varied one. For this reason it is advisable that in further research account be taken of different entrepreneur and enterprise-related factors (Aerts 1993). Certain important entrepreneur-related factors that play a part in the achievement of international success are: length of experience in the sector, language knowledge of the entrepreneur and/or his man-agers; and level of training of the entrepreneur (Donckels and Lam-brecht 1995). As far as the enterprise itself is concerned, it is certainly useful to take into consideration the sector and the more detailed size class in which the firm operates (Gallo 1993).

APPENDIX

Table 9A1 Significant coefficients and their (standard) errors

	Export	Import	Branch	Production plant	Taking licences	Giving licences	Joint venture
Quality of management	0.4037 (0.0871)	0.4057 (0.0871)					
Reputation and local image	−0.3054 (0.0767)	−0.2389 (0.0769)					
Worker skills							
Technology	0.2469 (0.0540)	0.1921 (0.0537)	0.1661 (0.0729)				
Product quality							
After sales service		0.2230 (0.0894)					
Creativity		0.1579 (0.0707)	0.1890 (0.0941)	−0.2390 (0.1184)			
Distribution and selling staff		0.2639 (0.0568)	0.3016 (0.0790)	0.2650 (0.1152)			
Product design		0.1808 (0.0677)	0.2304 (0.0879)				
Pricing policy			0.2228 (0.0841)				
Low cost level		0.2144 (0.0537)					
Market share		0.2776 (0.0655)					
Financial strength			0.1782 (0.0854)				
Customer relations	−0.2359 (0.0684)						
Flexibility							
Reliability of delivery							
Administration							
Product adaptation		0.2632 (0.0732)	0.2516 (0.1004)				

For the analysis we used logit regression. This technique is perfectly suited to estimate the value of a function for which the dependent variable is binary and can, therefore, assume two possible values.

The logistic curve can be described as follows:

$$\log y - \log(1 - y) = \alpha + \beta x$$

or

$$y = \frac{1}{1 + e^{-(\alpha+\beta x)}}$$

To estimate this curve we use the maximum likelihood method. The object of this technique is to determine α and β in such a way that the likelihood of generating the sample is maximized. Here no attention is paid to the determination coefficient (R2) for the evaluation of the estimate. The evaluation takes place as follows:

- examination of the signs of the estimated coefficients. A positive coefficient implies that when the value of the independent variable increases, the value of the dependent variable increases as well.
- examination of the significance of the coefficients by comparison of the estimated value with the standard error. By way of null hypothesis it is postulated that the relevant variable has no impact on the dependent variable, in other words, it is examined whether or not the estimated coefficient differs significantly from zero.

For more technical information, see Wonnacot, T.H. and Wonnacot, R.J. (1979) *Econometrics*, New York: John Wiley & Sons.

REFERENCES

Aerts, R. (1992) 'Becoming international: benefits and pitfalls for entrepreneurial SMEs. Experiences from Belgium', in the proceedings of the *RENT-VI Conference*, European Institute for Advanced Studies in Management, Barcelona.

Aerts, R. (1993) 'The influence of entrepreneur and SME characteristics on the perception of success factors in internationalization', paper presented at the *23rd European Small Business Seminar*, 15–17 September, Belfast.

Ali, A. and Swiercz, P. (1991) 'Firm Size and Export Behaviour: Lessons from the Midwest', *Journal of Small Business Management*, 2: 71–8.

Bamberger, I (1986) 'The Development of competitive advantage: theoretical bases and empirical results', Cahiers Stratégies et Organisation, University of Rennes.

Donckels, R. (ed.) (1993) *KMOs Ren Voeten Uit*, Brussels: Roularta Books, Koning Boudewijnstichting, KMO-Studiecentrum.

Donckels, R. and Aerts, R. (1993) 'Familiebedrijven onder de schijnwerpers' (Family-businesses in the spotlight), in R. Donckels (ed.) *KMOs Ten Voeten Uit* Brussels: Roularta Books, Koning Boudewijnstichting, KMO-Studiecentrum.

Donckels, R. and Fröhlich, E. (1991) 'Are family businesses really different? European Experiences from STRATOS', *Family Business Review*, 2: 149–60.

Donckels, R. and Lambrecht, J. (1995) 'Joint ventures: no longer a mysterious world for SMEs from developed and developing countries', *International Small Business Journal*, 2: 11–26.

Donckels, R. and Hoebeke, K. (1992) 'SME-led growth of the Belgian economy: fact or fiction?', *Entrepreneurship and Regional Development*, 4: 155–64.

Edmunds, S. and Khoury, S. (1986) 'Exports: a necessary ingredient in the growth of small business firms', *Journal of Small Business Management*, 4: 54–65.

European Network for SME Research (ENSR) (1993) 'The European observatory for SMEs', First Annual Report 1993, *EIM Small Business Research and Consultancy*, Zoetermeer.

Ferguson, W.G. and Gibb Y.K (1993) 'Internationalizing the small business. Helping SME overcome barriers to internationalization through resource based programmes', in the proceedings of the *23rd conference of the European Foundation for Management Development*, NISBI – The Small Business Institute, Belfast, 620–42.

Gallo, M.A. (1993) 'Internationalization of the family business', in M. Virtanen (ed.) *The Development and the Strategies of SMEs in the 1990s*, Helsinki School of Economics and Business Administration, Mikkeli.

Gallo, M.A. and Luostarinen, R. (1991) 'Internationalization: a challenging change for family businesses', *Proceedings of the 1991 FBN conference, IESE*, Barcelona: Universidad de Navarra, pp. 30–8.

Gallo, M.A. and Sveen, J. (1991) 'Internationalizing the family business: facilitating and restraining factors', *Family Business Review*, 2: 181–90.

Haahti, A.J. (ed.) (1993) 'INTERSTRATOS Internationalization of Strategic Orientations of European Small and Medium enterprises', *EIASM Working Papers 1–93*, Brussels.

Hanvey, E. (1993) 'The comparative performance of exporting and non-exporting small firms', paper presented at the *23rd European Small Business Seminar*, 15–17 September, Belfast.

Neubauer, H. (1992) 'The question of succession in family firms: planned continuity', paper presented at the *Recontres de St-Gall*, Swiss Research Institute of Small Business and Entrepreneurship, University of St.Gallen for Business Administration, Economics, Law and Social Sciences, St.Gallen.

O'Reilly, M. (1993) 'Exporting and the small firm: the Northern Ireland experience', in the proceedings of the *23rd Conference of the European Foundation for Management Development*, NISBI – The Small Business Institute, Belfast, 304–19.

Stratos Group, (1990) *Strategic Orientations of Small European Businesses*, London: Avebury.

Welsch, J. (1991) 'Family enterprise in the United Kingdom, the Federal Republic of Germany and Spain: a transnational comparison', *Family Business Review*, 2: 191–203.

10 Strategic management of British SMEs
Changes in attitude 1991–4

Graham Hall and Peter Naude

The strategic management of SMEs is an area of increasing interest to researchers, not least because virtually all firms fall into this category. Indeed it is large firms that are arguably the aberration. Interstratos surveys reveal the perceptions of SMEs' managers, usually owners, about various important aspects of strategy and how these perceptions have changed over time. Here we focus on three. First, the environment in which respondents operated, including how they performed in relation to other firms. Second, their reasons for undertaking overseas activity, or for not doing so (this section is based on responses to questions that were unique to the British survey). Third, the factors that were perceived as important for success.

Our results are derived from surveys carried out in 1992 and 1995 and refer to the previous years. Hence they provide insights into changes that occurred between 1991 and 1994, a period of turbulence that included the conversion of the European Union into a fully fledged Single Market. We are not able to disentangle the effects of the establishment of a Single Market from all of the other factors within the environment for SMEs that were also changing. We can say, however, that over the period considered overseas markets became more important to the populations of SMEs from which our samples were drawn. In 1991 the mean percentage of earnings from overseas activities amongst the 339 respondents was 13 per cent and the median approximately 2.5 per cent. In 1994 the mean amongst the 133 respondents was 23 per cent and the median 11 per cent.

Our results are presented as a simple survey. More sophisticated analysis of the data and the contribution which our results might make to academic controversy will be postponed to future publications.

FACTORS OF PRODUCTION

Respondents were asked about their experiences of the changes over the previous twelve months in the availability of various factors of production. In neither survey year did there appear to be a crisis in the supply of skilled manpower, with about half of respondents in both periods reporting no change and about 40 per cent an improvement, (i.e. that the change had been good or very good). This is surprising given the conventional wisdom that skill shortages are a constraint on the performance of the UK economy. Also surprising is the absence of change between years in the distribution of responses. Changes in the environment, not only the establishment of the Single Market but expansion of higher education, do not appear to have made any difference to the market for skilled labour.

In the market for unskilled labour there would appear to have been a slight deterioration in availability. A similar picture emerges with respect to the supply of young workers, though most striking is the consistency between periods of the approximately 60 per cent reporting no change, in spite of increases in youth unemployment and of the government initiatives to alleviate it.

In respect to the supply of raw and unfinished materials a significant decrease occurred in those reporting improvement and a similar increase in those reporting a deterioration, (i.e. that the change had been bad or very bad). On a lesser scale the same may be said of the supply of bought-in products for resale and the availability of equipment and know-how, though in both periods about half of the respondents reported no change having taken place.

In summary, between the survey years on the whole there does not appear to have been very much change in the conditions facing SMEs in their supply from the markets for their factors of production. Whatever the effects of the Single Market they have not been felt within these particular markets. Our findings are summarized in Table 10.1.

FINANCE

The adequacy of the capital market in meeting the needs of the SME sector has been a matter of debate for almost 70 years. Our results would suggest that in both periods about 40 per cent of respondents did not consider there had been any change in the availability of finance but in the latter period there was an increase in those reporting an improvement.

Table 10.1 Perceptions of changes in the availability of factors of production

Factors of production	Year	Very good	Good	Neutral	Bad	Very bad
Managers and skilled	1991	6	37	49	7	1
workers	1994	5	35	48	9	3
Unskilled workers	1991	6	36	50	6	2
	1994	3	31	60	6	–
Apprentices (including	1991	4	23	60	12	1
youths on training	1994	2	18	62	16	2
schemes)						
Bought in products	1991	7	39	50	4	–
for resale	1994	4	32	52	12	–
Equipment and	1991	7	44	47	2	–
know-how	1994	8	40	50	2	–
Raw and semi-finished	1991	7	48	39	5	–
materials	1994	–	31	43	23	3

Table 10.2 Changes over the previous twelve months in the capital market

	Year	Very good	Good	Neutral	Bad	Very bad
Availability of finance	1991	6	30	43	15	6
	1994	11	37	38	11	3
Availability and quality	1991	4	32	52	7	5
of financial advice	1994	11	39	43	6	2
Effects of interest rates	1991	2	5	19	41	33
	1994	5	32	47	15	2

The proportions that considered there had been no change in availability and quality of financial advice fell between surveys with commensurate increases in the proportions reporting an improvement. This presumably reflects the major marketing initiatives towards the SME sector from all the UK clearing banks. However, even in 1991, only a small minority judged matters to have deteriorated *vis-à-vis* financial advice.

Hardly surprising, the benefits from lower interest rates have been clearly perceived by respondents. Our findings are summarized in Table 10.2.

MARKET CONDITIONS

The markets in which the majority of SMEs must operate are characterized by inherent instability. Lacking the protection of the most potent barrier to entry, economies of scale, SMEs are far more vulnerable than large businesses to the threat from new competition. They may be able to exploit alternative barriers to those afforded by size, for instance their professional or technical skills or knowledge, but usually they must walk the treadmill of monopolistic competition. They may be able to maintain above normal profits through product differentiation, which can both prevent the erosion of demand and decrease its price elasticity, but as long as competitors potentially have the same options, they cannot do so indefinitely. Hence the need to react quickly to threats and opportunities that owners of SMEs commonly claim is necessary if they are to earn above minimum levels of profits, indeed even to avoid insolvency.

The single market in some ways made it easier for SMEs to sell abroad but, equally, could have left them more exposed to foreign competition in domestic markets. Respondents were asked about their experiences over the previous twelve months of changes in their volume of sales, their competitive position on various dimensions, and in the nature of their competition.

SMEs, lacking the muscle of size, are more vulnerable than large to the vagaries of relationships with customers and suppliers. Questions on perceptions of change in these relationships were also included in the surveys.

Volume of sales

There would appear to have been a decided upturn between periods in the levels of demand faced by respondents. The doubling of the proportion of respondents describing the change internationally in their sales over the previous twelve months as 'very good' may well be evidence of the benefits from the Single Market but the improvement in conditions within domestic markets was of, at least, the same order, suggesting a more general buoyancy in the SME sector. Matters appeared to have become better even in local markets (Table 10.3).

Table 10.3 Changes over the previous twelve months in the volume of sales

	Year	Very good	Good	Neutral	Bad	Very bad
Locally	1991	5	19	44	26	6
	1994	6	30	47	12	5
Nationally	1991	8	27	27	32	6
	1994	17	41	25	13	2
Internationally	1991	7	27	36	22	8
	1994	14	31	37	10	8

Competitive position

Respondents were asked about their perception of the change, over the previous twelve months, of the competitive position of their companies on three dimensions – price, quality and technology – and with respect to both domestic and overseas markets. As regards price, in 1994 about the same proportions reported a worsening of position within their domestic markets as an improvement. This suggests a strong variance in pricing behaviour. This impression is reinforced by the increase between periods in the proportions reporting both a worsening and improvement in conditions, albeit the latter was only slight.

In overseas markets the message is less ambiguous. In 1994 hardly any respondents reported a deterioration in their pricing position, whilst about 40 per cent regarded their position as having improved. Moreover, between periods there was a significant shift in the proportions reporting deterioration and improvement.

In neither periods did any significant number of respondents consider that the quality of their products had been lowered in comparison with those of competitors. Between periods there was some fall in the proportion reporting an improvement in the relative quality of their products in domestic markets with a commensurate increase in the proportion adopting a neutral position. Much the same inference might be drawn about the relative quality of products offered in overseas markets.

As regards both their domestic and overseas markets an increasing proportion of respondents believed the levels of technology they employed had improved in comparison with that of competitors. Within domestic markets the change was quite dramatic. In 1991 over

Table 10.4 Changes in competitive position

	Market	Year	Much worse	Worse	No Better	Better	Much Better
Price	Home	1991	4	17	53	24	2
		1994	2	25	44	27	2
	Overseas	1991	3	16	57	22	2
		1994	1	6	51	32	10
Quality	Home	1991	–	1	40	55	4
		1994	–	1	46	49	4
	Overseas	1991	1	–	46	51	3
		1994	–	–	51	42	7
Technology	Home	1991	2	56	38	4	–
		1994	–	4	46	46	3
	Overseas	1991	1	3	57	37	2
		1994	–	2	50	43	3

half of respondents reported a deterioration in their competitive position over the previous twelve months, with only a trivial number reporting an improvement. Four years later the ratio had practically been reversed. Our findings are summarized in Table 10.4.

Nature of competition

Respondents were asked about their perception of how the level of competition they faced had changed over the previous twelve months from small and large companies, and from UK and foreign companies, in all cases dichotomized between domestic and foreign markets. In five of the 16 rows in Table 10.5 half or more reported no change had taken place, in the remainder over 60 per cent. Both periods, therefore, were characterized by a large degree of stability in the levels of competition respondents faced from all quarters regardless of whether the markets were domestic or overseas. Furthermore, across the board, there was an increase in the proportion of respondents reporting an improvement in conditions and a decrease in those reporting a deterioration. Though there was variation in the changes in proportions there were no ready generalizations to be drawn about differences between domestic and overseas markets, or about whether changes in the level of threat faced were related to the size of competitors or to whether or not they were British.

Table 10.5 Changes in degree of competition

Type of firm	Market	Year	Much worse	Worse	No change	Better	Much better
Small firms	Home	1991	3	26	61	8	2
		1994	4	20	61	13	2
	Overseas	1991	6	32	51	10	1
		1994	2	12	73	11	1
Large firms	Home	1991	6	32	51	10	1
		1994	9	23	51	15	2
	Overseas	1991	5	22	66	6	1
		1994	3	15	66	13	2
UK firms	Home	1991	4	31	50	13	2
		1994	5	26	51	16	2
	Overseas	1991	1	17	73	7	1
		1994	–	12	74	13	2
Foreign firms	Home	1991	5	23	63	8	1
		1994	5	11	68	14	1
	Overseas	1991	4	24	62	8	2
		1994	2	20	64	11	3

Supplier and buyer power

Respondents were asked whether their negotiating position with suppliers and customers had changed in their domestic and overseas markets. In the both the UK and overseas markets the power of suppliers was perceived as having increased over the previous 12 months.

The situation within the two categories of market was not, however, the same. In both periods well over half of respondents reported no change in their negotiating position within overseas markets, as opposed to 36 per cent in both periods reporting no change in their relationship with domestic suppliers. The fall in the proportions reporting an improvement, and increase in the proportions reporting deterioration, were of a much higher order in the domestic than in overseas markets.

Relationship with customers would appear to have improved in both domestic and overseas markets but again conditions differed between the two. In both periods about a third of respondents reported no change in their relationship with UK customers but over half in their relationship with suppliers overseas. Therefore, as with relationships with suppliers, the overseas markets would appear to be far more stable. But the improvement in the domestic markets is somewhat stronger. Whilst the increase in proportions reporting this was about the same in both sets of markets the fall in the proportion reporting a deterioration in relationships is far more marked in the domestic. In 1991 over 50 per cent of respondents reported a deterioration against less than 40 per cent three years later. As regards relations with overseas customers the corresponding change was from 32 per cent to 19 per cent. Table 10.6 reports these findings.

Table 10.6 Changes in negotiating position

	Market	Year	Much worse	Worse	No change	Improved	Much improved
Suppliers	Home	1991	–	8	36	50	6
		1994	4	22	36	33	5
	Overseas	1991	2	8	60	30	–
		1994	2	18	55	25	–
Customers	Home	1991	5	50	33	11	1
		1994	5	33	36	24	2
	Overseas	1991	3	29	55	12	1
		1994	1	18	55	23	2

REASONS FOR UNDERTAKING OVERSEAS ACTIVITY

The question of whether to seek overseas earnings can clearly prove crucial to any firm, including an SME. There are a variety of reasons why firms may decide to operate outside their domestic markets and a variety of different reasons why they may not. Understanding both sets of reasons may facilitate the formulation of public policy initiatives to stimulate overseas activity and, where the relative importance of these reasons has changed, may provide some insight into the effects of the Single Market on the SME sector.

Firms earning more than 10 per cent of their sales from overseas activity were asked to indicate the importance of a set of factors that *a priori* might have played a part in their decision to sell overseas.

Size of home market

In 1991 almost half of respondents regarded as important (i.e. ranked as 'high' or 'very high') that their home market was perceived as too small, but three years later this had dropped to 36 per cent. This is surprising given that an effect of the establishment of the Single Market might have been expected to be to alter perceptions about the relative potential offered by British and European markets. See Table 10.7 for these findings.

Table 10.7 The home market was too small

Year	No importance	Low	Medium	High	Very high
1991	19	7	26	33	15
1994	15	18	30	21	15

Profit margins on exports

In 1991 a major reason for operating in overseas markets was the expectation of higher profit margins than would have been earned from domestic sales. Assuming there to be some validity in this expectation it could have arisen from differences between domestic and overseas markets in levels of demand, market structure and/or behaviour within markets. The validity of these explanations must remain open to conjecture. Similarly we do not know why this reason for undertaking overseas activity should have fallen in importance. The findings are reported in Table 10.8.

Table 10.8 Higher profit margin on exports

Year	No importance	Low	Medium	High	Very high
1991	14	11	29	32	14
1994	26	39	32	–	3

Security of customer base

In both periods reducing the risk from focusing on domestic markets alone represented a very significant motive for diversifying into overseas markets. In the absence of economics of scope this would imply that firms were prepared to earn a lower level of income in order to enjoy fewer fluctuations over time. There is some suggestion that this had fallen in importance between periods, perhaps reflecting the possibilty that domestic markets were perceived as having become more secure. The findings are reported in Table 10.9.

Table 10.9 To provide a more secure customer base

Year	No importance	Low	Medium	High	Very high
1991	5	4	14	55	23
1994	2	7	25	42	24

Initiatives from foreign customers or agents

Responses are spread fairly evenly over no/low importance, high/very high and medium effect of approaches from abroad, and the distribution displayed a remarkable consistency over time. It would seem that the overseas activities of respondents not uncommonly arose from explicit opportunities presented by potential customers, rather than resulting from a strategic decision to diversify overseas, and that the strength of these opportunities has not increased since the establishment of the Single Market. Table 10.10 reports these findings.

Table 10.10 As a result of initiatives from foreign customers or agents

Year	No importance	Low	Medium	High	Very high
1991	16	17	37	25	5
1994	14	20	37	27	2

Table 10.11 Their products are particularly appropriate for foreign customers

Year	No importance	Low	Medium	High	Very high
1991	63	22	9	5	1
1994	10	17	34	32	7

Belief in the attractiveness of products to foreign customers

There would appear to have been a considerable increase over time in the proportion of respondents who were motivated into overseas activity by the belief that their products would prove attractive to foreign customers. One might speculate that this indicates a new confidence about the quality of these products compared to those produced by overseas manufacturers. Table 10.11 reports these findings.

Personal experiences of decision makers

One might have expected that the greater part that Europe is playing in the domestic lives of the British managerial classes would have been reflected in the level of their commercial overseas activities, especially given that it is widely acknowledged that the strategic direction taken by SMEs is not uncommonly influenced by the personal circumstances of their owners and managers. The results of our surveys would not support this hypothesis. Indeed personal circumstances would appear to have assumed about the same, very low, level of importance in both periods. Table 10.12 reports these rather surprising findings.

Table 10.12 Personal circumstances (e.g. having worked abroad, family ties abroad)

Year	No importance	Low	Medium	High	Very high
1991	64	20	11	4	1
1994	61	18	14	4	2

Pure chance

A challenge to models premised on economic rationality is posed by those who emphasize the role of change in determining strategic behaviour. With almost half of respondents citing it as important in explaining their level of overseas behaviour the results of the 1991 survey would suggest that the part played by chance cannot be completely dismissed. However, three years later the proportion had fallen

Table 10.13 Pure chance

	No importance	Low	Medium	High	Very high
1991	13	15	24	31	17
1994	61	18	14	4	4

very dramatically, suggesting owners and managers feel more in control of the direction taken by their companies. See Table 10.13 for these results.

Encouragement/support from third parties in the UK

SMEs receive encouragement from a number of quarters to seek out export markets and this is often supported by various kinds of assistance. In 1991 this would appear to have had an impact on SME behaviour, with virtually half of respondents claiming third party encouragement to be important. In 1994 this had fallen to less than 10 per cent. This could be providing a message about the quality of assistance or, alternatively, the quality could have remained constant but was simply irrelevant in the latter period to the decisions taken by SMEs. Table 10.14 reports these findings.

Table 10.14 As a result of encouragement from third parties in the UK (e.g. trade associations, central government, local authorities, chambers of commerce)

Year	No importance	Low	Medium	High	Very high
1991	26	14	11	33	16
1994	41	42	8	7	2

REASONS FOR NOT UNDERTAKING OVERSEAS ACTIVITY

Firms that earned less than ten per cent of their revenue from overseas activity were asked why they had not sold more abroad.

Home market providing adequate opportunity

The proportion of respondents who claimed that they lacked the incentive to undertake overseas activity because they considered their home market provided sufficient opportunity stayed constant between periods at almost half. Given the undoubtedly formidable problems associated with attempting to conduct business overseas it is

Table 10.15 Home market provides sufficient opportunity

Year	No importance	Low	Medium	High	Very high
1991	15	15	24	31	15
1994	9	13	30	32	16

hardly surprising that SMEs will avoid this route if their domestic markets appeared adequate. Table 10.15 reports this finding.

Foreign markets are too competitive

The degree to which fear of competition represented a deterrent to undertaking overseas activity probably remained constant between periods in that about a quarter in both periods attached high or very high and about half low or no importance to this factor. A caveat to this, however, is that between periods there was a decided shift between 'no' and 'low' importance. Table 10.16 reports these findings.

Table 10.16 Foreign markets are too competitive

Year	No importance	Low	Medium	High	Very high
1991	27	23	25	23	2
1994	10	40	26	20	4

Limited knowledge of foreign markets

Lack of knowledge of overseas markets would appear, in both periods, to have served as a powerful constraint on attempts to operate within them. There is some suggestion that this lost importance between periods, but only slightly. Table 10.17 reports these findings.

Table 10.17 Limited knowledge of foreign markets

Year	No importance	Low	Medium	High	Very high
1991	15	9	24	37	15
1994	8	17	33	33	10

Lack of demand for our products

In both periods about a third of respondents believed the level of demand did not warrant attempting to sell in overseas markets. There

Table 10.18 Lack of demand for our products

Year	No importance	Low	Medium	High	Very high
1991	19	18	30	22	11
1994	6	40	18	28	8

is a suggestion that the proportion citing this as of low or no import-ance has increased but not sufficiently strongly to be able to draw any firm conclusions. This raises the question of why the importance of lack of demand should have remained about constant, in spite of the increase in the size of potential markets which might have been expected to have resulted from the establishment of the Single Market. Table 10.18 reports these disappointing findings.

Unable to meet technical requirements of overseas customers

Some clue as to the answer to the last question is perhaps provided by the increase in the proportion of respondents claiming that their ability to conduct business overseas had been hampered by their products not meeting the technical requirements of potential foreign customers. This might be construed as some reflection of the quality of their products *vis-à-vis* those of foreign competitors. This disturbing finding is reported in Table 10.19.

Table 10.19 Products do not meet technical requirements of foreign customers

Year	No importance	Low	Medium	High	Very high
1991	47	30	13	9	1
1994	6	40	18	28	8

Exporting is too risky

Overseas markets might be avoided because they are perceived as too risky and the importance of risk might have been expected to have changed over time either because the degree of perceived risk had changed or because of a change in respondents' attitude to that risk. In fact neither would appear to have occurred. In both periods almost half of respondents did not attach much, if any, importance to risk in explaining their decision not to undertake overseas activity whilst about a quarter did regard it as important. Fortunately this factor is not an insuperable problem for all as shown in Table 10.20.

Table 10.20 Too risky

Year	No importance	Low	Medium	High	Very high
1991	27	20	29	17	7
1994	23	25	25	19	8

Serious consideration given to exporting more

One reason for not undertaking a higher level of overseas activity might be that, for whatever reason, respondents had simply not considered doing so. Not all owner managers should be depicted as entrepreneurs, boldly seeking fresh opportunities in new markets. Some are deeply conservative about exploring the unknown and foreign markets might easily be regarded, in more than one sense, as quite alien. In both periods only a minority of respondents were prepared to admit this as important for their not conducting a high level of overseas activity and a half or more claimed it was of little or no importance. These findings are reported in Table 10.21.

Table 10.21 Had not seriously considered exporting more

Year	No importance	Low	Medium	High	Very high
1991	36	14	30	11	9
1994	29	29	16	18	8

Obstruction to exporting by foreign governments

The purpose of the Single Market was to remove restrictions on trade between European Union member states. Some of these would have been imposed by governments. It is surprising, therefore, that the proportion of respondents citing red tape from foreign governments as of no or low importance actually fell between periods. The reasons for this are not obvious. This disappointing finding is reported in Table 10.22.

Table 10.22 Red tape from foreign governments

Year	No importance	Low	Medium	High	Very high
1991	41	26	22	9	2
1994	20	32	34	6	8

Lack of contacts abroad

Between periods there was a significant drop in the proportion of respondents citing lack of contacts abroad for their low level of overseas activity and a significant increase in the proportion citing it as very important, but otherwise the picture has remained approximately the same. About half considered this of high or very high importance and about a quarter of low or no importance. These rather disappointing findings are reported in Table 10.23

Table 10.23 Lack of contacts abroad

Year	No importance	Low	Medium	High	Very high
1991	18	13	23	38	8
1994	4	20	25	29	22

Foreign language skills

The distribution of responses regarding the importance of lack of foreign languages has also displayed remarkable consistency over time. In spite of the generally acknowledged poor linguistic skills of British business people only about a third of respondents in either period considered that, in their cases, lack of languages had been an important reason for not selling overseas. The results shown in Table 10.24 are still disturbing, however.

Table 10.24 Lack of foreign languages

Year	No importance	Low	Medium	High	Very high
1991	24	26	21	18	10
1994	18	29	27	14	12

SUCCESS FACTORS

Respondents were asked to rate the importance for success of a variety of factors. It should be emphasized that responses can only be a reflection of respondents' perceptions and our results do not allow us to test their validity. However, perception of what is important, as seen through the eyes of owners, can provide insights into conditions within the SME sector, especially when comparisons can be made over time.

What is very striking is how little changed in the period between the surveys. In both surveys over 90 per cent of respondents claimed as important the quality of management in being able to respond quickly to the needs of customers/changing circumstances and reliability of delivery. Less than 50 per cent regarded as important, in either period, the following factors: local reputation; charging the lowest possible prices; large capital reserves; public relations; and, somewhat surprisingly, trading in Europe.

Table 10.25 Perceptions of factors important for success

Factor	Year	No importance	Low	Medium	High	Very high
Quality of management	1991	–	–	8	41	51
	1994	–	1	5	42	52
Local reputation	1991	12	19	20	29	20
	1994	14	23	22	25	16
Skills of workforce	1991	–	2	23	46	28
	1994	–	3	18	45	34
Keeping up to date with technology	1991	1	10	34	36	19
	1994	2	5	30	38	25
Ability to solve technical problems	1991	2	7	25	37	29
	1994	2	8	22	34	34
After sales service	1991	4	9	19	32	36
	1994	1	8	9	40	42
Creativity	1991	5	15	29	28	23
	1994	2	14	31	33	19
Quality of sales force	1991	4	5	15	43	31
	1994	1	2	21	42	34
Design of the product	1991	8	6	17	35	34
	1994	5	6	16	40	33
Charging lowest possible prices	1991	9	21	38	20	12
	1994	3	23	44	17	13
Achieving lowest possible costs	1991	–	4	18	42	36
	1994	2	5	17	36	40
Gaining market share	1991	1	6	24	46	22
	1994	2	5	22	43	28
Large capital reserves	1991	6	29	40	17	8
	1994	8	30	39	18	5
Public relations	1991	6	20	33	26	16
	1994	8	19	38	22	14
Being able to respond quickly to customer or changing circumstances	1991	–	–	9	41	50
	1994	–	–	9	40	51
Reliability of delivery	1991	–	–	4	36	60
	1994	–	–	4	31	65
Sound administration	1991	–	–	14	58	28
	1994	–	–	15	61	24
Ability to modify products	1991	4	9	25	42	18
	1994	5	9	32	35	19
Trading with European countries	1991	18	24	25	20	13
	1994	14	25	27	22	12

There is a hint that the skill of the workforce, keeping up to date with technology and after sales service gained in importance but this may be stretching the information value of our data to the point of heroism. Table 10.25 summarizes our findings on perceptions.

CONCLUDING REMARKS

Our results would lead us to be fairly optimistic about some aspects of what is happening in the SME sector. On the whole, responses suggest stability or even improvement in the environment around the sector. Markets, domestic and local, as well as overseas, would appear buoyant and responses suggested an increase in confidence over various dimensions of competitiveness.

Similarly there was some suggestion that those respondents who carried on business overseas, did so increasingly because of their perceptions about the suitability of their products for overseas markets. Chance appears to have become less important over the period considered, and personal circumstances/experiences of owners and managers continue to be perceived as still not of importance. The latter is a little surprising as British managers are supposedly becoming more European in their private lives. Even more surprising the perceived adequacy of domestic markets does not appear to have been reduced, in spite of the expectation that the establishment of the Single Market would have opened up new possibilities. The influence of third party initiatives, which would include those from government, would also appear to have waned, which should not escape the notice of public policy makers.

Public policy to encourage overseas activity no doubt must take into account the reasons why it is not undertaken. Limited knowledge of overseas markets and lack of contacts were important in both periods, suggesting scope for public policy initiatives, though satisfaction with the size of domestic markets also remained important, which can probably be less readily altered by such initiatives.

Perceptions of factors leading to success maintained a striking consistency between survey periods. Not surprisingly, quality of management was regarded as of high importance in both periods but very surprising was the comparatively low importance attached to low prices. Perhaps the management of SMEs, unlike the former Conservative government, have grasped the elementary axiom of strategy that it can prove fatal to their firms, and if not fatal almost certainly not very profitable, to attempt to occupy niches that require they should be ultra competitive on price.

Index